Alex Scarrow

When Seconds Count

By Alex Sachare

a **SPORTS**MASTERS book
SPORTS PUBLISHING INC.
WWW.SportsPublishingInc.com

Director of Production, Book Design: Susan M. McKinney
Cover design: Scot Muncaster
Proofreader: David Hamburg

ISBN: 1-58382-015-9

A SportsMasters Book
SPORTS PUBLISHING INC.
804 N. Neil
Champaign, IL 61820
www.sportspublishinginc.com

Printed in the United States.

For Lori and Debbie, the loves of my life.

Acknowledgments

The author is indebted to Tom Bast of Sports Publishing Inc., who conceived and helped mold this project, as well as to Dale Ratermann of the Indiana Pacers for his support.

Many newspaper and magazine articles, books and Internet sites were used as source material for this manuscript. Among the many valuable books were the *Official NBA Guide and NBA Register*, edited by Mark Broussard, Craig Carter, Mark Bonavita and Brendan Roberts; *The Official NBA Basketball Encyclopedia*, edited by Alex Sachare; *The NBA Finals* by Roland Lazenby; *Tall Tales* by Terry Pluto; *Ever Green* by Dan Shaughnessy; *Drive* by Larry Bird with Bob Ryan; *Red Auerbach, An Autobiography* by Arnold "Red" Auerbach and Joe Fitzgerald; *Hondo* by John Havlicek with Bob Ryan; *Giant Steps* by Kareem Abdul-Jabbar and Peter Knobler; *Kareem* by Kareem Abdul-Jabbar with Mignon McCarthy; *A View From Above* by Wilt Chamberlain; *They Call Me The Big E* by Elvin Hayes and Bill Gilbert; *Magic's Touch* by Earvin "Magic" Johnson Jr. and Roy S. Johnson; *Change the Game* by Grant Hill; *America's Dream Team* by Chuck Daly with Alex Sachare; *The Chicago Bulls Encyclopedia* by Alex Sachare; *A Coach for All Seasons* by Morgan Wooten and Bill Gilbert; *From Orphans to Champions* by Morgan Wooten and Bill Gilbert; *Hoosier Hysteria* by Bob Willians; *Hoosiers: Classified* by Bob Hammel; *A Sense of Where You Are* by John McPhee; *Inside Sports: College Basketball* by Mike Douchant; *50 Years of the Final Four* by Billy Packer with Roland Lazenby; and *The Encyclopedia of the NCAA Basketball Tournament* by Jim Savage. All are recommended and worth hunting down for a more in-depth look at specific events that are described here. Among the many useful websites were nba.com and wnba.com; cnnsi.com;

sportingnews.com; finalfour.net; and sites for individual colleges, which often may be found with the suffix .edu.

Thanks also to Bob Rosen of the Elias Sports Bureau, Dennis D'Agostino of the New York Knicks, John Gillis of the National Federation of State High School Athletic Associations and the sports information offices of Southern California, Duke and Texas Tech for their assistance.

Table of Contents

Acknowledgments iv

Introduction x

00:59: "Havlicek Stole the Ball!" 1

00:58: Jordan Goes Out In Style 6

00:57: North Carolina Slays Goliath In 3 OTs 9

00:56: Robinson's Free Throws Give Michigan the Title 13

00:55: Dr. Naismith's "Athletic Distraction" 17

00:54: Lisa Leslie Scores 101 Points – In A Half! 21

00:53: Anderson's Misses Open the Door For Rockets To Sweep 24

00:52: Bird Picks Pistons' Pockets 27

00:51: Allen Feeds Big Dog, Who Take Bite Out of Philadelphia 31

00:50: Allagaroo! CCNY Doubles Its Pleasure 33

00:49: Arizona Beats the Best En Route To 1997 Title 38

00:48: Boston's Comeback Kids 41

00:47: San Antonio's Little General Comes Up Big 44

00:46: Wilt Scores 100! 48

00:45: Spanich Hits Two Three-Pointers In Less Than One Second 52

00:44: Jerry West: "Mr. Clutch" 55

00:43: Celtics Win First Title, But Just Barely 59

00:42: Bob Pettit's Revenge 64

00:41: The Real-Life *Hoosiers*: Milan High School 68

00:40: Selvy's Memorable Miss 72

00:39: Gonzaga Wears the Slipper With Attitude 76

00:38: Magic Fills In For the Big Fella 78

00:37: Sampson Stops the Lakers 82

00:36: The Birth of the NBA 86

00:35: Imhoff Carries Cal to Title 90

00:34: Francis Tops, Selvy Hits Century Mark 94

00:33: Notre Dame Stops UCLA's Streak at 88 97

00:32: How A Tennis Racket Helped DeMatha Beat Power Memorial ... 100

00:31: Showdown in the Astrodome: Houston Beats UCLA 103

00:30: Cheryl Miller Leads Southern Cal to Title—With Flair **107**

00:29: It's Miller Time! 110

00:28: The New York Knicks' Miracle Finishes 114

00:27: Slick Leonard Lifts Indiana Over Kansas 118

00:26: Hoosier Hysteria: Bailey Leads Bedford to State Title 121

00:25: Larry Bird and Magic Johnson: A Rivalry For All Time 124

00:24: The Shot Clock That Saved the NBA 128

00:23: Jordan Hits "The Shot" 132

00:22: Armstrong Weaves His Magic 136

00:21: Bradley, Russell Duel at Madison Square Garden 140

00:20: Bird vs. Wilkins: Shootout in Boston Garden 143

00:19: Auerbach, Cousy, Russell All Go Out Winners 147

00:18: Indiana Gets Smart 151

00:17: Princeton's Amazing Comeback 154

00:16: Charlotte Smith Beats the Clock 158

00:15: Jordan's Jumper, Worthy's Steal Give Smith His First Title 161

00:14: N.C. State's Charles Dunks Phi Slamma Jamma 165

00:13: Henderson's Steal Saves the Celtics 168

00:12: When Villanova Could Do No Wrong 171

00:11: Loyola Stops Cincinnati's Run 175

00:10: Cheryl Swoopes To the Hoop 178

00:09: T-Spoon's Miracle Slows Comets, Can't Stop Their Three-Peat 181

00:08: Yes, UConn! 186

00:07: The One and Only Dream Team 189

00:06: The Olympic Game That Ended Three Times 195

00:05: The Greatest Game of All Time? 198

00:04: Carlisle's Second Effort Wins NIT For California 203

00:03: Paxson Nails the Three-Peat 206

00:02: Magic Borrows Kareem's Shot 209

00:01: Laettner's Miracle Shot Beats Kentucky 212

Introduction

Basketball is a game of speed and excitement, of spirited rallies and fabulous finishes. It is truly a game where every second counts, where the very rules of the game have been changed and refined to help teams mount late charges and come from behind to win, or at least make it close. In basketball, with its shot clocks and three-point arcs, virtually no lead is safe until the final buzzer has sounded.

This book counts down some of the most amazing comebacks, improbable rallies, fantastic feats and astounding buzzer-beaters the game has ever seen. It puts you in the middle of the fast-paced, heart-stopping action, as teams play catch-up, trying to milk every second to cut into a lead. It takes you into the huddle, as teams set up last-second, game-winning shot attempts. And it puts these plays in context, describing the drama and setting the stage for some of basketball's most dramatic moments.

There is no shortage of material from which to draw. The fact is, buzzer-beaters happen every night, every season. Whether it's an NBA star sinking a game-winning jumper he's practiced thousands of times or a high school kid having her prayer from beyond mid-court answered, these shots happen whenever and wherever the game is played.

This should not be surprising. The rules of basketball encourage competition, and devices such as time limits on how long a team may hold the ball, extra points for shots made beyond a certain distance and restrictions on the types of defense which may be played all work toward producing closer games. What's more, between the pros, colleges and high schools, men and women, boys and girls, there are tens of thousands of games played every year in the United States alone, to say nothing of the rest of the world, where basketball is the fastest-growing sport around. So there is ample opportunity.

In this book we've tried to present many of the best-known game-winning shots and great comebacks that have taken place in over 100 years of basketball history, as well as a few less widely known buzzer-beaters from the most recent seasons that illustrate how these plays can and do happen nightly. This book is not encyclopedic or all-encompassing, nor is it meant as an "all-time greatest" list, because any such effort would be impossibly subjective. Every fan has his or her favorite comeback and most memorable shot, and obviously, not all of them are in here.

This book is meant as a sampling of some of the great plays, memorable moments and fantastic finishes basketball has to offer. We hope you enjoy *When Seconds Count.*

00:59

"Havlicek Stole the Ball!"

John Havlicek scored 26,395 points in 16 seasons with the Boston Celtics and another 3,776 in 13 trips to the playoffs—more than 30,000 points in all. Yet he is best remembered for none of them, but rather for a steal he made just before the end of a game in the 1965 NBA Playoffs.

Havlicek's play was immortalized by the late Johnny Most, the long-time radio play-by-play man of the Boston Celtics whose gravelly voice brought the Celtics' dynasty to life for millions of fans throughout New England. Most's call of that play ranks right up in the sports pantheon with Russ Hodges' *"The Giants win the pennant! The Giants win the pennant!"* from baseball's 1951 National League playoffs or Al Michaels' *"Do you believe in miracles?"* from the USA hockey team's gold medal win at the 1980 Olympics.

The play took place in the closing seconds of Game 7 of the Eastern Conference Finals between the Celtics, who had won the previous six championships, and their arch-rival Philadelphia 76ers, who had been strengthened by the midseason addition of the imposing Wilt Chamberlain to a roster that already included Hal Greer, Chet Walker and Luke Jackson. Although Philadelphia took just a 40-40 record into the playoffs, it clearly was a team that was getting better each day as Chamberlain adjusted to his new teammates.

The Celtics had won a league-high 62 games with a unit that featured Bill Russell, Sam Jones, K.C. Jones, Tom Heinsohn, Satch

Sanders, Willie Naulls and Havlicek, in only his third pro season but already regarded as the premier sixth man in the NBA. Boston coach Red Auerbach had pioneered the concept of the sixth man, the guy who could come off the bench and perk up the team when the starters began to sag. He used Frank Ramsey effectively in that role early in the Celtics' run of 11 championships in 13 seasons from 1957 through 1969. But Ramsey had retired in the summer of 1964, and now the job belonged to Havlicek.

A terrific athlete who was drafted by the Cleveland Browns of the National Football League as a wide receiver even though he never played football in college, the 6-foot-5 Havlicek had played in the shadow of Jerry Lucas, a three-time All-American and two-time college Player of the Year at Ohio State. It was Lucas who dominated that team, averaging 24.3 points and 17.2 rebounds a game from 1960 through 1962. Havlicek was the defensive stopper, the player whose job was to contain the opposing team's scoring star so Lucas could focus on his own offense. As a result, Havlicek's statistics were modest, 14.6 points and 8.6 rebounds per game—he wouldn't average 20 ppg until his fifth season in the NBA. But Auerbach loved his versatility, his athleticism and his team orientation and selected Havlicek in the first round of the 1962 NBA Draft.

By the 1964-65 season, Havlicek had stepped into Ramsey's role as sixth man, backing up scoring leaders Sam Jones at guard and Heinsohn at forward. He played nearly 29 minutes a game and ranked second on the team in scoring (18.3 ppg), fifth in rebounding (4.9 rpg) and fourth in assists (2.7 apg). Steals were not yet being kept as an official NBA statistical category.

Boston, as Eastern Division champion, had a bye through the first round of the playoffs while third-place Philadelphia defeated second-place Cincinnati 3-1 in the best-of-five first round. In the division finals, the home team won each of the first six games, with the deciding Game 7 at Boston Garden. And that one went down to the closing seconds, with Boston trying to hold off a Philadelphia rally that had cut the Celtics' lead to five points, then three, then finally one at 110-109 with five seconds to play.

All Boston needed to do was pass the ball inbounds and run out the clock, but that proved far easier said than done. Russell tried to inbound the ball from under his own basket, but it hit one of the wires that ran down from the ceiling of Boston Garden and helped support the backboards. Referee Earl Strom called it a violation and awarded possession to Philadelphia.

"When Russell inbounded the ball and hit the guy wire," recalled Havlicek, "I don't think anyone thought that we weren't going to be able to get the ball back again and be able to inbound it. All of a sudden there was this controversy and the ball was given back to Philadelphia."

"I called Russell for throwing the ball and hitting the wire," said referee Earl Strom, who 30 years later would be inducted into the Basketball Hall of Fame. "The call had to be made. That was a court rule, like a ground rule of the arena."

During the ensuing timeout, Philadelphia coach Dolph Schayes thought about getting the ball to Chamberlain, but also wanted to have another option. "Wilt's problems at the foul line weighed on my mind, so I set up a play where Hal Greer would pass the ball to Chet Walker, and Johnny Kerr would set a pick to free Walker for a shot," said Schayes.

In the Boston huddle, Russell, who had just turned the ball over, asked his teammates for help. "Russell came into the huddle and said, 'Man, somebody bail me out. I don't want to be wearing those horns,'" said Havlicek.

Given one last chance to pull out victory with five seconds on the clock, Greer took the ball from the referee under the basket and first looked toward the 7-1 Chamberlain in the low post. But the smaller, quicker Russell moved in front of Chamberlain, making a pass into the pivot too risky. Meanwhile, K.C. Jones was leaping along the baseline and frantically waving his arms to distract Greer.

"I knew they had five seconds to put the ball in play," said Havlicek. "My thought was, as the official handed Greer the ball, to start counting, 'one thousand one, one thousand two, one thousand three.' Generally a pass is made within the first second or two, and I knew that he was having some sort of problem because that guy wire was in the exact same position as where Russell had inbounded it. So it may have been a thought on his mind, too."

With Chamberlain covered, Greer looked for an alternative. To get a better view of the court, he jumped up and spotted Walker out beyond the key. But Havlicek, the savvy defender, had taken a position several feet off the direct line of sight between Greer and Walker, making it look like Walker was open when really he wasn't.

"When he was having trouble putting it in play," said Havlicek, "I sort of had a vision as to where the ball was and where my man was, and I started to peek a little. When I got to 'one thousand four' and the ball still hadn't been passed in, I took a peek over my shoulder and saw that Greer was about to lob a pass to Walker. I knew that it wasn't a good pass and that I would have a good chance of deflecting or intercepting it. I made a controlled deflection to Sam Jones, who was right near me. He went down the sideline dribbling out the clock and the game was over. As soon as the buzzer went off, the crowd went bananas.

"The incident would have ended right there and would be remembered as just one of the many big things the Celtics have been involved with," added Havlicek, "except that our announcer, Johnny Most, went almost completely haywire at the end of the game. He had established a reputation as an excitable broadcaster long before that night, but something about the drama of this particular ending really hit him and he launched into one of the most famous spiels in Boston sports broadcasting history."

Printed words don't do it justice—you have to imagine Most starting tentatively, then getting excited and finally losing it. Here is his call:

"Greer is putting the ball into play. He gets it out deep," Most intones. Then suddenly his voice rises in a frenzy: *"Havlicek steals it. Over to Sam Jones. Havlicek stole the ball! It's all over! Johnny Havlicek stole the ball!"*

"It was hysteria and euphoria," said Havlicek. "Fans were grabbing me and a couple of fans ripped off my jersey. Years later, I went to a party and a woman came up to me and showed me this brooch she had. She asked me if I recognized the material. I didn't. She told me it was a piece of my uniform that someone had gotten that night."

Havlicek lost his jersey, but the Celtics had the win, and would go on to capture their seventh consecutive championship, beating the Lakers in five games.

"John Havlicek was a great scorer and a great competitor," said teammate Heinsohn. "He was a winner in every sense of the word. He loved the pressure situation and he loved to come through, particularly on defense. He's one of the all-time great defensive players."

And his defensive gem against Philadelphia will never be forgotten, thanks to Most's magical call.

"I didn't realize it was that outstanding a play until I heard Johnny Most," Havlicek later said. "The next day, radio station WHDH, which did our games in those days, kept repeating the tape of the game ending, including Johnny Most's semi-hysterical ending. All over Greater Boston, the phrase "Havlicek stole the ball" meant a great deal. The play has gotten bigger as time goes on."

00:58

Jordan Goes Out in Style

Michael Jordan always had style, and a sense of timing.

He burst onto the global basketball scene with a game-winning shot against Georgetown that gave North Carolina the 1982 NCAA championship, and he left with a game-winning shot against Utah that gave the Chicago Bulls the 1998 NBA championship. That last on-court image of Jordan is a fitting one by which he should be remembered: Jordan going one-on-one, faking Bryon Russell off balance and firing his jumper, arm extended in the classic shooter's follow-through.

Whether or not there have been others who rate up with Jordan when it comes to that magical combination of skill, will to win and grace under pressure can be debated, but it is beyond question that there have been none who rate higher. If ever there was a player who was made for that one shot, game on the line, winner take all, it was Michael Jordan.

That was the situation Jordan and the Bulls were in on June 14, 1998, when they faced the Utah Jazz in Game 6 of the NBA Finals. The Bulls, seeking their third consecutive championship and sixth in eight years (Jordan missed all of one and most of the second of the two non-championship seasons due to his brief retirement and foray into baseball), had grabbed a 3-1 lead in the best-of-7 series but had failed in an attempt to close it out at home when Utah pulled out an 83-81 win in Game 5.

That had been a bad game for Jordan, the 1998 NBA Most Valuable Player who shot just 9-for-26 from the field, and a good one for Karl Malone, the 1997 MVP who had been an early-series disappointment but who had broken out with 39 points and nine rebounds for Utah in Game 5. "I would have loved to have won it here at home," said Jordan. "That would have been a great scenario."

Instead, the teams boarded their charter flights and headed west to Salt Lake City, where Game 6 (and a possible Game 7) would be played before the rabid Jazz fans at the Delta Center. Utah had finished the regular season with a 62-20 record, the same as Chicago's, but earned the home-court advantage by winning both head-to-head matchups.

Jordan still was thinking of the missed chance represented by Game 5, but could put it in perspective. "We blew our opportunity," he said, "but this has happened to us before. It's a duplicate situation as in 1993."

That year, when the Bulls also were going for a three-peat, they failed to close out the Finals at home by losing Game 5 to the Phoenix Suns. But Chicago went to Phoenix's America West Arena and beat the Suns 99-98 in Game 6 on John Paxson's dramatic three-pointer with 3.9 seconds to play.

Little did Jordan know just how closely this game would parallel the 1993 situation.

Just as the Suns had five years earlier, the Jazz gave Chicago all it could handle throughout the game, and when John Stockton nailed a three-pointer with 41.9 seconds left, Utah went ahead 86-83. The prospect of a Game 7, with momentum on Utah's side, suddenly was very real. But Jordan wouldn't allow it to happen.

He took the inbounds pass and drove down the right lane, scoring in remarkably easy fashion as just 4.8 seconds ticked off the clock. That assured Chicago, now trailing by one, of getting the ball back without having to foul and put Utah at the free-throw line. The Jazz tried to work the ball to Malone in the low post, but Jordan sneaked in on a double-team and knocked it away, then came up with the loose ball.

Rather than call a timeout, which would have given Chicago a chance to discuss a final play but also would have allowed Utah to set up its defense, the Bulls elected to keep playing and pushed the ball into the frontcourt, where Jordan took it to the left of the key. He noticed, on the fly, that teammate Steve Kerr was set up on the left wing and knew that Stockton could not afford to leave the Chicago marksman unguarded. That meant Bryon Russell would be left to guard him one-on-one, or until someone else could come over from the other side of the court to help.

Jordan made sure such help would not arrive in time. In a blink of an eye he made his move, stutter-stepping as Russell reached for the ball and then driving past him toward the middle of the court, with Russell off balance and struggling just to stay on his feet.

"When Russell reached, I took advantage of the moment," said Jordan. "I never doubted myself. I never doubted the whole game."

As Russell scrambled to recover, Jordan used his left shoulder, arm and hand to maintain enough space between himself and the defender, then elevated for his 18-foot jumper. It sailed through the net with 5.2 seconds remaining, giving Chicago an 87-86 lead and Jordan 45 points on the night. Following a timeout, Stockton attempted a three-pointer that bounced off the rim and time expired as the teams chased down the rebound. Chicago had its repeat three-peat.

"Great money players, no doubt about it," Coach Phil Jackson said of his Bulls, but thinking of one in particular. "That was the best performance I've seen in a critical situation and critical game in a series. Michael is one of the great sharks. When the game is on the line, he wants to win."

00:57

. . . .

North Carolina Slays Goliath in 3 OTs

"Nobody roots for Goliath," Wilt Chamberlain was fond of saying, and North Carolina coach Frank McGuire may have had that in mind when he sent his team out for the opening tip of the 1957 NCAA championship game against Chamberlain and the Kansas Jayhawks.

McGuire sent 5-foot-11 Tommy Kearns out to jump center for North Carolina against the 7-foot-1 Chamberlain. "I told him if he jumped high enough, he might reach Wilt's stomach," McGuire said. "You're not going to get the tap anyway, so why waste a big man? Wilt looked freakish standing there, so far above our man. Wilt looked 10 feet tall towering over Tommy, but they made such a ridiculous picture together that Chamberlain must have felt no bigger than his thumb—at least, that was the state of mind we wanted him to get into."

"We all had a little chuckle," said North Carolina star Lennie Rosenbluth, "and it just took all the tension out of the game."

McGuire was confident that his Tar Heels, unbeaten to that point, were better than Kansas at every other position, so he focused everything, physically and psychologically, on containing Chamberlain, the sophomore center who had led Kansas to a 24-2 record. Chamberlain was the subject of his pre-game talk to his team.

"I said he was so good, maybe we had better not show up," McGuire related. "I said he might stuff some of them through the basket with the ball. I said we didn't have a chance unless our entire team defensed him at all times, and he'd still probably beat us so bad it would be embarrassing to go home. Of course, I was kidding them and they knew it, but it was psyching them up and loosening them up at the same time."

Not that the Tar Heels, who had beaten Michigan State 74-70 in three overtimes in the national semifinal, necessarily needed it. "We're a chilly club—I mean, we just keep cool," Kearns said. "We play it chilly all the time. Chamberlain won't give us the jitters like he did to all those clubs."

"As we got ready for the game, we tried to remember that no matter if he dunked the ball over his head or whatever, it was still just two points," said Rosenbluth. "It counts the same as hitting a little jump shot from 10 feet out, so we tried not to be awed."

Needed or not, McGuire's talk, and his opening ploy, had the desired effect.

"I think Wilt was taken aback, as I think the whole team was," said Kearns. "It set a tone for the game, and we jumped off to a very big lead as a result. I think it was a daring move by Coach McGuire, and it had an awful lot to do with us winning the game."

North Carolina jumped out to a 9-2 lead, and Chamberlain didn't get his first basket until nearly five minutes had gone by. With the Tar Heels collapsing around Chamberlain, they extended the margin to 19-7 after 10 minutes before the Jayhawks began to come back, closing to 29-22 at halftime.

North Carolina had shot .647 from the field in the first half, with the All-American, Rosenbluth, scoring 14 points, and 6-9 center Joe Quigg scoring from the corner when Chamberlain wouldn't come out after him. But Dick Harp, Kansas' first-year coach who had been an assistant to the legendary Phog Allen before Allen reached the mandatory retirement age of 70, knew his team could come back with Chamberlain in the lineup.

"Don't panic," he declared at halftime. "Play your game. We'll catch them."

It took Kansas just four minutes to wipe out the deficit, and midway through the second half, the Jayhawks had inched ahead 40-37. Rosenbluth fouled out with 1:45 remaining and Kansas still in front 46-43 on Gene Elstun's three-point play off a feed from Chamberlain. It looked like Allen's brash preseason prediction, "We could win the championship with Wilt, two sorority girls and two Phi Beta Kappas," might come true.

But a basket by Quigg cut the margin to one, and after Ron Loneski misfired on the inbounds pass, Kearns was fouled and sank the free throw with 20 seconds left to send the game into overtime, tied 46-46.

Both teams played slowdown in the overtime, getting one bucket apiece. Bob Young, Rosenbluth's replacement, scored for North Carolina, while the Kansas basket was scored by Chamberlain, who also blocked a last-second shot attempt by Kearns.

Neither team scored in the second overtime, which was enlivened when Chamberlain and North Carolina's Pete Brennan got into a scuffle. Chamberlain had been fouled by Bobby Cunningham, and Brennan had grabbed him around the waist at the same time.

Chamberlain threw the ball away and elbowed Brennan in the head, and both benches quickly cleared. Police had to come onto the floor to help the referees restore order.

Kearns hit a layup to open the third overtime and added two free throws for a 52-48 lead, but Chamberlain's three-point play and a free throw by Maurice King tied the score. North Carolina tried to play for the final shot, but Kansas' John Parker stole the ball from Quigg and fed Elstun, who was deliberately fouled by Kearns. Elstun made one of two free throws, putting Kansas ahead 53-52 with 31 seconds left.

On the ensuing play, Kearns tried to drive the lane but had his shot attempt rejected by Chamberlain. The carom came to Quigg at the top of the key and he too tried to drive to the basket. His shot also was batted away by Chamberlain, but King, trying to help out on the play, fouled Quigg with six seconds left on the clock, sending him to the line for two free throws.

McGuire called a timeout. "Now Joe, as soon as you make 'em," he began his pep, then instructing his players on how to defend a last Kansas effort. For his part, Quigg said he often had dreamed of winning a big game, "only in my dream, it was a jump shot with no time left."

As the team broke the huddle, assistant coach Buck Freeman told Quigg, "Follow through and end up on your toes." That's where he ended up both times, and both free throws were good to give North Carolina a 54-53 lead. A last-ditch pass intended for Chamberlain was tipped away by Quigg and recovered by Kearns, who dribbled once and then threw the ball straight into the air. Time expired before it came down, and North Carolina had its second straight triple-overtime victory—and a national championship.

Chamberlain had scored 23 points, but Rosenbluth had 20 and three other North Carolina players scored in double figures. Nevertheless, McGuire—who later would coach Chamberlain in the NBA, including the game in which he scored 100 points—paid tribute to the young giant when the game was over.

"We played him, not Kansas," he said. "We beat Kansas, not him."

00:56

. . . .

Robinson's Free Throws Give Michigan the Title

Sometimes a basketball player has to take things into his own hands. Larry Bird once stood silently in a Boston Celtics huddle for more than a minute before turning to his coach and saying, "Just tell them to give me the ball and get out of the way."

That's how Michigan guard Rumeal Robinson felt during the closing seconds of the 1989 NCAA championship game against Seton Hall. Regulation play had featured a remarkable shootout between Michigan's Glen Rice, who finished with 31 points, and Seton Hall's John Morton, who led all scorers with 35. Robinson's reverse, over-the-head dunk had given Michigan a 51-39 lead with 14:17 to play, but Seton Hall battled back and tied the score 71-71 on Morton's three-pointer with 24 seconds left in regulation. The game went into overtime after Rice failed to connect on a jumper shortly before the buzzer.

Another three-pointer by Morton midway through the overtime put Seton Hall ahead 79-76, but the Pirates failed on two chances to increase the spread when Morton missed a layup and Gerald Greene missed the first free throw in a one-and-one situation. After Michigan center Terry Mills cut the gap to one with a jumper, Seton Hall isolated Morton against Robinson, but his driving six-footer missed the rim and Michigan rebounded with seven seconds to play.

Michigan coach Steve Fisher—an assistant who had stepped up to the head job on an interim basis just before the start of the NCAA tournament when coach Bill Frieder signed to coach Arizona State and Michigan decided to let him move on immediately rather than after the season—had told Robinson not to call a timeout, no matter what happened on the Pirates' possession. The idea was to strike quickly, before Seton Hall had a chance to get back on defense. If a three was needed, go for the three; otherwise, take whatever you can get.

Although Rice—"Once I get on a roll, I feel like I can't miss," he said—figured to be the man to take the last shot, he never got his hands on the ball. Robinson decided to keep it and make the play himself. He dribbled the length of the court and penetrated down the lane, and with three seconds left, drew a blocking foul on Seton Hall's Greene.

"I didn't want to put the burden on anyone else's shoulders," Robinson said of his decision to try to make the last play himself. "I've been hiding on last-second shots. I decided if anyone took it, I wanted to be the one. I was either going to shoot or get fouled. It was a little cockiness, but mostly confidence."

Even though he was only a 64 percent foul shooter, Robinson stepped up to the line and nailed both free throws, giving Michigan an 80-79 lead. Seton Hall couldn't get off a good shot in the little time remaining, and the Wolverines—who had needed a last-second put-back by forward Sean Higgins to beat Illinois 83-81 and reach the finals—were national champions.

Earlier in the season, in a similar situation, Robinson had missed two free throws. So he did something about it. "For two weeks straight, he came in an hour early and shot a minimum of a hundred free throws every day," said Fisher. That extra work paid off in the end.

"It is a childhood dream to do something like this," said Robinson, who was born in Jamaica and came to the United States when he was six. "I don't know whether to cry or not. You cherish the good times, but where I come from, you remember the hard times."

Michigan's final month qualified as good times, hard times and tumultuous times, all rolled into one. "Life's crazy," mused Fisher, the first interim coach ever to take a team to the Final Four, much less the national title. "I'm just happy to be on the ride."

Robinson's free throws completed a remarkable three-week run for Fisher, who stepped into the shoes of a man who had posted seven consecutive 20-win seasons and was known as one of the game's premier recruiters, though he'd never led the Wolverines to the Final Four. Frieder had assembled a Michigan team that had size and skill and so many good shooters that it led the nation in field goal percentage at .566. But the Wolverines seemed like underachievers —they could do no better than a third-place finish in the Big Ten Conference, and they lost their regular-season finale to conference rival Illinois by 16 points.

That's when word of Frieder's negotiations with Arizona State surfaced. Though the agreement was for Frieder to take over Arizona State following the conclusion of the NCAA Tournament, Michigan did not like the idea of a lame-duck coach leading its team into the postseason. Michigan athletic director Bo Schembechler, the former Wolverine football coach, told Frieder he could start at Arizona State immediately and turned the team over to Fisher, his mild-mannered assistant for the past seven years.

Fisher, who had never been a college head coach before, did more than just take over Frieder's players and run Frieder's plays. He spoke with each of his key players and made sure they knew what was expected of them in each game. As for Rice, the team's most explosive scorer, Fisher told him he expected him to pick up his game in the tournament, and as a sign of his confidence he said he would make Rice the first option on every play Michigan ran.

This communication seemed just the right touch for a team of talented players that had never quite lived up to expectations under Frieder. It certainly had the desired effect on Rice, who, following a regular-season loss to Indiana, had told his teammates that they all were "going on a mission" that would only be fulfilled with a national championship.

"For as long as I can remember," said Michigan center Loy Vaught following the win over Seton Hall, "we've decided to go on this mission, and now the mission has been accomplished."

Rice had a brilliant NCAA Tournament, scoring 184 points in six games to break the record of 177 points set by Princeton's Bill Bradley in 1965 (in five games). His 31-point effort against Seton Hall made him the Big Ten's all-time leading scorer with 2,442 points, surpassing Michigan's Mike McGee, who scored 2,439 points. He was voted the Most Outstanding Player of the tournament.

"He loaded all of us up and took us to the Promised Land," said Fisher, who had the interim tag removed from his coaching title following the tournament.

But they would not have gotten there had Robinson not taken matters into his own hands, forced the issue on the final possession of the overtime and made two clutch free throws to beat Seton Hall.

00:55

. . . .

Dr. Naismith's "Athletic Distraction"

There always has been a time element in basketball, ever since the game was invented by Dr. James Naismith, a Canadian-born instructor at the YMCA Training School (now Springfield College) in Massachusetts in 1891.

Unlike baseball, where an inning can go on for as long it takes to record three outs, a basketball game ends after a predetermined amount of time. The only thing that can prolong it is if the teams are tied when that time limit is reached; then they play an overtime period of a specific length to determine the winner, or additional overtimes if the score remains tied.

So in that sense, seconds always have counted in Dr. Naismith's game. Just how many seconds, however, has varied.

NBA games are 48 minutes long, broken into four 12-minute quarters. That's 2,880 seconds, if you want to think of it that way. College games, as well as games in the WNBA and in countries outside the United States, are 40 minutes (2,400 seconds) long, divided into two 20-minute halves. High school games usually are 32 minutes (1,920 seconds) long, consisting of four eight-minute quarters.

The first basketball game ever played, as it happens, was 30 minutes long, divided into two 15-minute halves. There was only one basket scored in the entire game, a 25-foot toss by a young man named William R. Chase. The score of that first game was recorded as 1-0, and Chase will forever have the honor of having scored the first game-winning basket in history.

In a way, the cold New England weather can be blamed for the invention of basketball. Dr. Luther Gulick, head of the physical education department at the YMCA school, asked Naismith to devise an "athletic distraction" that would keep students busy during the winter time. It had to be played indoors, because of the frigid, snowy weather in New England, yet it had to provide for enough activity to permit students to burn off excess energy.

Naismith considered taking popular outdoor games like soccer and lacrosse and moving them indoors but rejected that idea as too dangerous. He wanted a game that was similarly active, but not quite as violent. So he thought back to his days as a student at McGill University in Montreal, where he had helped the school's rugby players stay in shape during the winter by having them run and flip a ball into a box set up on the gymnasium floor. He also remembered an outdoor game called Duck on a Rock that he had played as a child, where competitors tossed small stones at larger ones set up as elevated targets. By combining the two, he had the basis for his new game—players, divided into two teams, would run around the gym floor and try to toss a ball into an elevated target.

The concept of the target being elevated was vital. Naismith wanted his game to promote agility, finesse and eye-hand coordination rather than brute force; speed and skill rather than strength. The target had to be off the floor and above the players' heads.

The first game of basketball was played on December 21, 1891, according to 13 rules written up by Naismith and posted on the gymnasium wall. The gym was 50 feet long and 35 feet wide, so those became the dimensions of the first basketball court (barely over half as long and two-thirds as wide as today's standard NBA or college court, which measures 94 feet by 50 feet). There were 18 students in Naismith's gym class, so the teams in the first game ever played had nine on each side.

As for the elevated targets, again Naismith adapted to his surroundings. The gym, as did many in that era, had an elevated running track encircling it, so Naismith decided to have the targets hung from there. The track happened to be 10 feet above the floor—the same height at which baskets are set in most levels of the game today.

Balls were no problem, as the school had plenty of soccer balls which could be used. Targets were another matter. Naismith asked the custodian of the gym, Pop Stebbins, to get a pair of boxes that were a little bit bigger in diameter than a soccer ball and nail them to the running track. But Stebbins couldn't find any boxes that were the right size; instead, he returned to the gym with a pair of round peach baskets. Naismith went along with the idea, and thus the game became "basket ball" rather than "box ball" (and "hoops" rather than "squares").

Actually, Naismith's students wanted to call the game "Naismith ball," after its creator, but the modest instructor wouldn't permit it. Thus it became known as "basket ball," and over the years the two words were shortened to one.

Not much is known about that first game, other than that Chase scored the only basket. However, when the students left school for their winter holiday, they took the new game with them to their hometowns. Thus the game quickly spread throughout the East Coast and as far west as Chicago; within a year it had crossed international boundaries, since five of Naismith's students in that first game were from Canada and one from Japan.

Here are some more firsts from basketball's early history:

• The first game between teams from competing organizations was a 2-2 tie played on February 12, 1892, between the Central YMCA and the Armory Hill YMCA, both of Springfield. Why didn't they play overtime? Nobody knows. Maybe they did, and it stayed tied till both teams finally decided to go home.

• The first game to draw spectators was one month after that, when the Springfield YMCA Training School students defeated the faculty before some 200 fans.

• The first women's game was played between two classes at Smith College in Northampton, Massachusetts, on March 22, 1893. Senda Berenson Abbott, the director of physical education at Smith, met with Naismith to learn about the game and brought it to her school.

• Students at Yale, Stanford and Geneva (Pennsylvania) College were playing the game as early as 1892, but the first game between a college team and an outside opponent came in January 1893, when the University of Toronto beat the Toronto YMCA 2-1.

• The first intercollegiate games on record took place in 1895, when Minnesota A&M beat Hamline 9-3 and Haverford beat Temple 6-4. Precise dates are unavailable.

• The first intercollegiate women's game took place on April 4, 1896, when Stanford defeated California 2-1. In deference to the modesty of the times, no men were permitted to attend—and when two men had to enter the gym to fix one of the baskets, it was reported that "the Berkeley team screamed and hid in a corner."

• The first professional game that can be documented took place in Trenton, New Jersey, in 1896, when a group of players who couldn't use the local YMCA rented the local Masonic Hall and charged admission to defray expenses, agreeing to split any profits. The game was a success and each player took home $15 after expenses were covered. There was $1 left over, and that went to the Trenton team captain, Fred Cooper, who thus became the first "highest paid player" in basketball history.

00:54

• •

Lisa Leslie Scores 101 Points—in a Half!

There has been at least one game where seconds didn't count much at all.

It took place on February 7, 1990, between Morningside High School of Inglewood (California) and South Torrance High School of Torrance (California).

Lisa Leslie of Morningside made the clock an afterthought as she scored 101 points—in the first half alone! That's 101 points in 16 minutes of basketball. Breaking it down, it comes to more than six points per minute, or one point every 9.5 seconds. Those numbers have never been equaled at any level of organized basketball, men's or women's.

"That was a game I'll never forget," said Leslie. "I wasn't keeping track of my points or anything, but my teammates kept passing me the ball and telling me to score. The team we were playing really wasn't very good and didn't have anybody my size, so I just kept shooting."

By halftime, South Torrance had seen, and been shot at, enough. The team refused to play the second half, considering it pointless and embarrassing.

Leslie, a 6-foot-5 center, went on to play college ball at Southern Cal, leading the Lady Trojans to four NCAA Tournament berths and averaging 20.1 points and 10.1 rebounds in her 120-game career. She set Pac-10 career records for scoring (2,414 points) and rebounding (1,214 boards) and also the USC records for blocked shots in a season (95) and a career (321). She was the consensus National Player of the Year as a senior and was named All-America as both a junior and senior. She's the only player in Pac-10 history to receive All-Conference first-team honors four times.

After playing one season professionally for Siligesso in Italy, where she averaged 22.6 points and 11.7 rebounds, Leslie joined the USA Basketball Women's National Team that practiced together for a year and then won the gold medal at the 1996 Olympic Games in Atlanta. Leslie was the USA's leading scorer at 19.5 ppg and second-leading rebounder at 7.3 rpg.

She then signed with the WNBA and was assigned to the Los Angeles Sparks. Leslie averaged 15.9 ppg and 9.5 rpg in 1997, then improved to 19.6 ppg and 10.2 rpg in 1998, when she led the league in rebounding and double-doubles (16) and ranked third in scoring.

Leslie, who also has worked as a model and a sports television reporter, has had a brilliant, highlight-filled basketball career for a person who had to be repeatedly persuaded to even try the game. Despite the advantages of her height (she was 6 feet tall in the seventh grade), she didn't like the game at first, but finally decided to give it a try. Her cousin, Craig, served as her personal coach, working with her in various basketball drills and urging her to compete against boys as well as girls in order to improve her skills. Obviously, the hard work and effort paid off.

However, Leslie was denied a chance at setting the all-time girls' basketball single-game scoring record when the South Torrance team didn't come out for the second half. She finished four points short of the record of 105 points, set by Cheryl Miller of Riverside Polytechnic High School against Norte Vista High School in Riverside, California, on January 26, 1982. (The boys' record belongs to Danny Heater of Burnsville, West Virginia, High School, who scored 135 points in a game on January 26, 1960.)

Miller is a member of the Naismith Memorial Basketball Hall of Fame in Springfield, Massachusetts, which represents all levels of the game and has been inducting women since 1984. It's an honor that is all but certain to eventually be accorded to Leslie, but players are not eligible for induction until five years after their retirement.

Another Hall of Fame member, Nancy Lieberman-Cline, was the first woman to play in a men's professional league, competing in the summer United States Basketball League for the Springfield Fame in 1986 and the Long Island Knights in 1987. She also has played for the Washington Generals, the team that competes against the Harlem Globetrotters. In addition, she has played in several women's professional leagues and is now coaching in the WNBA.

Yet another Hall of Famer, Ann Meyers, attended training camp with the NBA's Indiana Pacers in 1979. Meyers, a four-time All-American at UCLA and a silver medalist in the 1976 Olympics, worked out with the Pacers in preseason but did not make the team's roster, at least partially because she's only 5-foot-9.

"From a fundamentals standpoint, Ann is excellent," said Bobby Leonard, the Pacers' coach at the time. "Some of the guys had better thank God that she doesn't have about six more inches and 40 more pounds."

No woman ever has played or coached in the NBA, although the league does have female referees. In 1977, the then-New Orleans Jazz selected All-American Lucy Harris of Delta State, a future Hall of Famer, in the seventh round of the NBA draft, but she never joined the team.

00:53

·························

Anderson's Misses Open the Door for Rockets to Sweep

In the last 10.5 seconds of Game 1 of the 1995 NBA Finals, Nick Anderson of the Orlando Magic attempted four free throws. He missed them all, and the Houston Rockets went on to win the game in overtime and sweep the Magic en route to the NBA championship.

Those misses not only altered the course of the series, but the future of the Orlando franchise. Had Anderson made even one of those shots, the Magic almost certainly would have beaten the Rockets in Game 1, momentum would have been on their side, and who knows how the rest of the Finals would have played out? It's hardly inconceivable to think that Orlando couldn't have gone on to win the title.

Take it a step further: With a championship ring on his finger, would Shaquille O'Neal have bolted for the Los Angeles Lakers when he became a free agent in July, 1996, or might he have stayed in Orlando to anchor the Magic? Might Brian Hill, Orlando's coach when the team reached the Finals, still be at the helm of the Magic instead of with the Vancouver Grizzlies, who signed him after he was fired by Orlando in February 1997? And might Anderson and

Penny Hardaway, both traded by Orlando in the summer of 1999, still be with the team as well?

The Magic had the home-court advantage in the 1995 NBA Finals and came out smoking, building a lead of 20 points in the first half of the series opener. But Houston, the league's defending champion, weathered the storm and refused to panic. By halftime the Rockets trailed by just 11, then Kenny Smith got a hot hand in the third quarter and sank a Finals-record five three-pointers as Houston outscored Orlando 37-19 to lead 87-80 going into the fourth quarter.

Then the pendulum swung the other way and Orlando came back, first erasing the deficit, then moving in front in the final minute. The Magic led 110-107 when Houston was forced to foul and Anderson stepped to the line with 10.5 seconds left. Making just one of the free throws would have put the Rockets in a deep hole, but he missed both. The rebound, however, was tipped around and finally recovered by Anderson, who again was fouled. Once again he stepped to the line and missed both free throws, and this time Houston gained possession. With 1.6 seconds on the clock, Smith nailed his record seventh three-pointer of the game to tie the score and force overtime.

"When you get to that point in a close game," said Hill, "all the little things jump up and bite you, and tonight for us it was free-throw shooting. We let one get away from us."

Houston held the upper hand in the five-minute extra period before Dennis Scott sank a three-pointer for the Magic with 5.5 seconds remaining, tying the score at 118-118. On the ensuing possession, Houston's Clyde Drexler drove down the lane, forcing the Orlando defense to react. As O'Neal moved over to pick him up, Drexler tossed the ball up onto the backboard. Houston center Hakeem Olajuwon, having been left alone by O'Neal, had a clear path to the basket and tipped in the offensive rebound with three-tenths of a second showing on the clock, giving the Rockets a 120-118 victory.

The capacity crowd of 16,010 at the Orlando Arena was stunned into silence. "It got so quiet, I didn't realize the basket was in," said Olajuwon, who tallied a game-high 31 points.

When Game 2 began, Orlando seemed to still be feeling the effects of its failure to close out the series opener. The Magic fell behind by 22 points at halftime and Houston cruised to a 117-106 win. The Rockets had gone to Orlando and taken the first two games of the series, and when they returned home, forward Robert Horry drove another nail into the coffin by sinking a three-pointer with 14 seconds remaining to give Houston a 106-103 victory and a 3-0 series lead. Three nights later, Houston got 35 points and 15 rebounds from Olajuwon and nailed the coffin shut with a 113-101 victory. It was only the sixth 4-0 sweep in the 49-year history of the NBA Finals.

After Game 1, Anderson spoke about keeping his failure to come through in the clutch in proper perspective. "I've been in worse situations," he said. "My high school teammate (Ben Wilson), I watched him die. He got shot twice in the stomach and I saw it. I was right there, no more than 25 feet away. You grow up on the streets of Chicago, you can see anything. Wednesday night (Game 1) was not a tragedy, it's just something that happens. It was just basketball."

Although he claimed to have put his Game 1 failure behind him, Anderson's game went south. He shot just 9-for-32 from the field and 3-for-6 from the foul line during the remainder of the series, and was a non-factor in the Magic's next three losses. His troubles continued the following season. After averaging 15.8 points per game in his first seven seasons in the NBA, he averaged just 12.0 ppg in 1996-97. More noticeably, his field-goal percentage dropped from a career mark of .465 to .397, and his free-throw percentage plummeted from .695 to .404. It took him a full season to regain his confidence; in 1997-98 he was just about back to normal, averaging 15.3 ppg while shooting .455 from the field and .638 from the line.

The Rockets became the lowest-seeded team to win an NBA championship, having gone into the playoffs as the sixth seed in the West after a 47-35 regular season. En route to the title they beat four teams, each of which had won at least 50 games: the Utah Jazz (60-22), the Phoenix Suns (59-23), the San Antonio Spurs (62-20) and the Orlando Magic (57-25).

"It's hard for me to put into words how I feel about this team," said Rockets coach Rudy Tomjanovich. "The character, the guts—no team in the history of the league did what this team did. Every team we beat could have won the championship.

"We had nonbelievers all along the way, and I have one thing to say to those nonbelievers: Don't ever underestimate the heart of a champion."

00:52

Bird Picks Pistons' Pockets

Time was catching up with the Boston Celtics. The team that had won NBA championships in 1981, 1984 and 1986 was, by 1987, beginning to feel the effects of infirmity and age. But when you have the basketball instincts and ability of a Larry Bird or a Dennis Johnson, sometimes you can hold back the clock.

Kevin McHale had suffered a broken navicular bone and torn ligaments in his right foot during the 1986-87 season, and although doctors feared he could do further damage, he elected to keep on playing in hopes of a repeat championship. Bird was just starting to feel the pain in his back that, five years later, would end his playing career. The bench, one of the team's strengths in its run to the 1986 title, had been decimated by foot injuries to Bill Walton and Scott Wedman, who combined to play in just 16 games in 1986-87 and none after that.

In addition, by the start of the 1987 NBA Playoffs center Robert Parish was 33 years old, Johnson was 32, and the starting five averaged a shade over 30.

But the Celtics were not about to cede the title of the NBA's Team of the Decade for the 1980s to the Los Angeles Lakers, who had won championships in 1980, 1982 and 1985. Not without a fight, anyway.

Nor were they ready to give up their position as the Beast of the East, the dominant force in the Eastern Conference, even though the young and hungry Detroit Pistons were lapping at their heels.

The Celtics won the Atlantic Division title in 1986-87 with a 59-23 record, the best in the Eastern Conference. Atlanta had won the Central Division at 57-25, finishing five games ahead of Detroit, but the surging Pistons knocked off the Hawks in five games in the Conference Semifinals to set up a showdown against Boston.

Detroit was a young, deep and tough team that featured the brilliant backcourt trio of Isiah Thomas, Joe Dumars and Vinnie Johnson, high-scoring Adrian Dantley at small forward, future "Bad Boys" Bill Laimbeer and Rick Mahorn at the power positions and a pair of energetic rookies, Dennis Rodman and John Salley, for frontcourt depth.

The teams split the first four games of their best-of-7 series, the home team winning each, but Detroit's wins came more easily, including a 26-point rout in Game 4. The Pistons had momentum on their side when they came into Boston Garden for Game 5, and they matched everything Boston could throw at them for nearly 48 minutes.

With the Pistons coddling a 107-106 lead in the final minute, Rodman blocked a driving shot attempt by Bird. Thomas and Boston's Jerry Sichting tried to get the loose ball, but it squirted out of bounds and was awarded to Detroit with five seconds on the clock. All the Pistons had to do was get it inbounds and run off five seconds, and they'd be going home with a chance to end the series at the Palace of Auburn Hills. Detroit coach Chuck Daly tried to call a timeout to make sure his team was under control, but the ball was at the far end of the court and none of the Pistons could see him or hear him amidst the cacophony of the Garden, so play continued.

As Thomas prepared to inbound the ball from the sideline deep in the Boston frontcourt, Bird looked away from his man and stole a glance at Thomas just as the Pistons' captain peered toward Laimbeer in the low post. Anticipating the pass, Bird moved into the passing lane and stole the ball just before it could reach Laimbeer's hands.

"I saw Laimbeer open down low and I automatically headed toward him," Bird said. "Isiah lobbed one to Laimbeer. At the last instant, I reached in and just barely tipped it. I was trying to get control of the ball while practically falling out of bounds on the left baseline and I was just getting ready to throw it up when I saw a blur, a white jersey streaking down the lane. The blur was Dennis Johnson."

Johnson, who Bird often called the best player he ever played with, had been above the foul line but instinctively cut to the basket when he saw Bird go for the steal. Instead of attempting a hurried, off-balance shot, Bird fired a pass to Johnson, who caught it and laid it in with one second remaining to give Boston a 108-107 victory.

Here is the call of the play by Boston's radio voice, Johnny Most, who started slowly as Thomas had the ball and then moved into a frenzy when Bird picked it off:

"Aaaaaannnnd ... now there's a steal by Bird! Underneath to D.J., who lays it in! We might have one second left. What a play by Bird! Bird stole the inbounding pass, laid it off to D.J. and D.J. laid it in and Boston has a one-point lead with one second left. Oh, my, this place is going crazy!"

"If D.J. hadn't made the cut down the lane, we would have been dead ducks," said Bird. "I couldn't get my feet positioned right. I didn't really want to have to shoot it, but there wasn't much time left, so I would have had to. D.J. reacted perfectly. A lot of players would still be standing there."

One of the measures of greatness is the ability to bring out the best in your teammates. There is no question that Bird brought out the best in teammates like Johnson with his feel for the game and how it should be played.

Bill Fitch, Bird's first coach with the Celtics, perhaps described his basketball instincts best when he said, "Larry's mind takes an instant picture of the whole court. He sees the creative possibilities."

Although Detroit regrouped to win Game 6 at home 113-105, the Celtics captured Game 7 at the Garden 117-114 and advanced to the NBA Finals for the fourth year in a row. The Lakers would prove to be too much, however, winning in six games.

That victory over the Pistons was the last golden moment for this Celtics squad, which lost its Eastern Conference title to Detroit in a six-game series in 1988, was eliminated by the Pistons in the first round in 1989 and hasn't made it past the second round of the playoffs in the past decade.

00:51

· ·

Allen Feeds Big Dog, Who Takes Bite out of Philadelphia

When they had a chance to atone for a misconnection that had cost the Milwaukee Bucks a shot at victory two nights earlier, Ray Allen and Glenn "Big Dog" Robinson made the most of it—although they cut it as closely as possible.

There was just one-tenth of a second left on the game clock when Robinson's baseline jumper off a feed from Allen went through the net, capping a Milwaukee comeback from a 12-point second-half deficit and giving the Bucks a 93-92 victory at Philadelphia on February 16, 1999.

Allen and Robinson, the Bucks' two young stars, had been in a similar situation two days earlier at Orlando, but Allen's pass to Robinson had been tipped away, denying the Bucks a chance at a go-ahead basket in the closing seconds of a game the Magic went on to win 85-82.

"Ray made up for it tonight," said Robinson.

"I had the same opportunity in Orlando and I made a terrible pass. I rushed it and made a bad decision," said Allen, whose pass was knocked away by the Magic's Horace Grant. Orlando recovered and iced the victory with a pair of free throws by Darrell Armstrong.

Mistakes, however, can prove valuable, provided you learn from them.

"This time," said Allen, "I had an opportunity to break my man down. I was trying to shoot the ball, but G was standing there, wide open."

The Bucks had trailed most of the game, going all the way back to 7-6 early in the first quarter. Then again, it doesn't matter who leads along the way, it's who's ahead at the buzzer that counts.

"This game had a lot of weirdness to it," said Bucks coach George Karl. "It was just one of those games where I kept yelling, 'Hang around.' We weren't doing a lot of things better than Philly, but we just kept hanging around."

And when you hang around long enough, good things can happen.

Philadelphia, which led by 14 points during the second quarter and by 12 at 64-52 midway through the third quarter, saw its lead cut to one point several times in the closing minutes. Terrell Brandon's three-pointer brought Milwaukee to within 88-87 with 3:18 left, but Allen Iverson responded with two free throws for Philadelphia. Brandon's 15-footer cut it to 90-89, but Harvey Grant (twin brother of Horace, who had thwarted the Bucks two days earlier) responded with a five-footer to put Milwaukee back up by three with 47 seconds left.

Milwaukee went for a quick shot and Robinson missed, but Tyrone Hill was there to clean the offensive glass and his putback made it 92-91. On Philadelphia's next possession, the Sixers worked the clock down before Iverson drove into the lane but missed a five-footer. Brandon grabbed the rebound and called a timeout with 14.5 seconds left, giving Karl a chance to set up a final play.

Allen inbounded the ball to Brandon, who tested the perimeter before giving Allen a return pass. Allen drove into the lane between Eric Snow and Aaron McKee and kicked the ball out to Robinson, standing all alone on the left baseline. George Lynch tried to race over and get a hand in Robinson's face, but was too late. Big Dog's jumper already was in the air and headed for the basket.

Philadelphia coach Larry Brown wasn't upset with the shot, but with the way his young players had responded to Allen's drive and left Robinson wide open. "Everybody on that team could have made that shot," said Brown.

Especially Robinson, the college basketball Player of the Year in 1994, the first player chosen in the NBA Draft and a career 20+ ppg scorer after five pro seasons. Robinson never got his hands on the ball in Orlando for a chance at a game-winning basket, so he jumped at the opportunity against Philadelphia.

"It was a little different this time," said Robinson. "Tonight Ray Allen penetrated and got to the hole. That sunk my man in (toward the basket) and gave me a good look. I thought Ray was going to shoot it, but I kept my hands ready because I was open."

00:50

• •

Allagaroo! CCNY Doubles Its Pleasure

You may know what a Hoya is, but what's an Allagaroo?

To refresh your memory, when all Georgetown students were required to study Greek and Latin, the university's teams were nicknamed "The Stonewalls." It is believed that a student used Greek and Latin terms to come up with the cheer "Hoya Saxa!" which means "What Rocks!" Gradually, all Georgetown teams became known as "Hoyas."

Allagaroo is the start of the distinctive cheer for the City College of New York, which in 1950 accomplished something no school ever did before, nor has done since, nor is likely to do in the future —win the championships of both the National Invitation Tournament and the National Collegiate Athletic Association Tournament in the same season.

"Allagaroo-garoo-garah,
allagaroo-garah;
eee-yah, eee-yah,
sis-boom-bah!"

But what, precisely, does "Allagaroo" mean? Some say it's a cross between an alligator and a kangaroo. The romantics on campus, however, prefer to say it stems from the French phrase *allez guerre,* which means "to the war"—which makes sense considering all the military parlance in sports. Teams "fight" for victory, games are "hard-fought battles," a home run or long pass or three-point shot is a "bomb" and so on.

In the spring of 1950, "Allagaroo!" became the battle cry of New York, as CCNY, the school that prides itself as the "working man's Harvard" by offering a quality, free (since changed to reasonably priced) education to all residents of the city, climbed to the top of the basketball world. Coached for three decades by Hall of Famer Nat Holman, a player on the great Original Celtics team from the barnstorming era, CCNY featured a 6-4 senior, Irwin Dambrot, and four sophomore starters—Floyd Layne, Ed Warner, Al "Fats" Roth and 6-6 Ed Roman.

In those days, the NIT at New York's Madison Square Garden was still a major event, regarded on a par with the NCAA Tournament and played two weeks before the NCAA tourney began so teams could compete in both. But losses to upstate rivals Canisius, Niagara and Syracuse in the second half of the season put CCNY's hopes for any postseason play in jeopardy, until victories over intra-city rivals NYU and St. John's cemented its NIT bid.

CCNY started strong, beating defending champion San Francisco 65-46 in its opener and then routing Kentucky 89-50 in the quarterfinals. This was a Kentucky team, coached by Adolph Rupp, that had won the NCAA title the previous two seasons and featured a 7-foot sophomore center, Bill Spivey. Holman moved his center, Roman, away from the basket, where his shooting touch wouldn't be threatened by Spivey, and shifted the 6-3 Warner into the pivot, where his array of fakes and moves often negated the Kentucky player's height advantage. Warner wheeled around Spivey for 26 points and keyed a fast-break attack that overwhelmed Kentucky, dealt Rupp the most lopsided loss of his career and served notice that CCNY was a team to watch.

Next up for CCNY was Duquesne, and the Beavers' 62-52 victory not only moved them into the NIT final but also earned them a berth in the NCAA Tournament. The selection committee had been unable to pick from among CCNY, Duquesne and St. John's and had decided to award a spot in the Eastern Regional to the team that got the farthest in the NIT. When CCNY defeated Duquesne in one semifinal and St. John's bowed to Bradley in the other, the berth belonged to the Beavers.

First up was the NIT final against Bradley, the top-ranked team in the nation with a 29-3 record and an All-American forward, Paul Unruh. With Holman coaching despite a 103-degree fever, CCNY came back from an early 11-point deficit to trail by just 30-27 at the half, then pulled in front in the second half and won 69-61 behind 23 points by Dambrot.

"The team just seemed to arrive in the Kentucky game," said Holman, who spent the time between the NIT victory and the start of the NCAA Eastern Regional, conveniently scheduled for Madison Square Garden, recuperating from his fever. "I don't think they have been lucky and I don't think they've just been hot. They simply found themselves. And if they stay hale and hearty, I think we can beat anybody, and that includes Bradley again."

Since 1939, when the NCAA Tournament was inaugurated, four teams had entered both events. Three had won one tournament but been beaten in the other. CCNY was trying to become the first to win both, and among those teams in the field was Bradley, a late addition to the Western Regional. In the meantime, however, CCNY's players remained students first, athletes second, as Layne was reminded when he was roused from a daydream by a professor in a bacteriology class with a curt, "Mr. Layne, the game was played last night. Now look at the slide and tell me what you see."

CCNY opened the NCAA Tournament against second-ranked Ohio State, led by 6-5 All-American Dick Schnittker. After a 40-40 first half, the Beavers decided to shorten the game, at one point taking more than four minutes off the clock in the second half without even attempting a shot, and emerged with a 56-55 victory when the Buckeyes' Jim Remington missed a shot with five seconds left.

Next came North Carolina State, which trailed 38-37 at halftime. Sam Ranzino scored 16 of his 24 points in the first half of the second period for the Wolfpack, but fouled out with 3:30 to go. That was the edge the Beavers needed, and with Warner getting two baskets in the last 1:35 and Layne adding two free throws, CCNY had a 78-73 win and a berth in the finals. Meanwhile, Bradley beat UCLA and Baylor to secure the other spot in the NCAA finals and a chance to avenge its loss to CCNY only two weeks earlier.

This time it was CCNY that got in front early, leading 39-32 at the half and 58-47 with 10 minutes left. At this point Bradley scrapped its zone defense and went to a full-court, man-to-man press, and when Roman fouled out a minute later, the Braves started to get back into the game. They still trailed 69-63 with 57 seconds remaining, but a free throw by Joe Stowell and a layup, a steal and another layup by Gene Melchiorre brought Bradley within one. Then Melchiorre made another steal and drove in for what would have been the go-ahead basket, only to have it blocked at the last moment by Dambrot, who picked up the loose ball and fired it downcourt to Norman Mager, the team's sixth man.

Mager, who had been knocked unconscious in a collision with Bradley's Aaron Preece late in the first half and had needed five stitches to close a two-inch gash in his forehead but returned to action wearing a large bandage, caught the court-length pass and scored the clinching basket with less than 10 seconds left. CCNY had a 71-68 victory and its second national title in just over two weeks.

"No college team will ever duplicate this fabulous achievement," said Hall of Fame coach Clair Bee of Long Island University in a Garden filled with cries of "Allagaroo!" Half a century later, no team has, and right now it's impossible since the tournaments are run simultaneously.

Less than a year later, four prominent CCNY players were indicted in a point-shaving scandal that hit other schools including Bradley and Kentucky. Holman was forced to resign (although he later was cleared of any wrongdoing and reinstated), and the team had to move its games from the Garden and downgrade the basketball program. So the glorious run to two national championships in 1950 remains CCNY's shining basketball moment.

00:49

. . . .

Arizona Beats the Best
En Route to 1997 Title

After only finishing fifth in the Pac-10 Conference, the young Arizona Wildcats found their stride at the right time and beat three top-seeded teams to win the 1997 NCAA championship, capping their remarkable run by knocking off defending national champion Kentucky 84-79 in overtime in the title game.

It marked the first time that a club had beaten three No. 1 seeds since the regional seeding process was begun in 1979.

Throughout the tournament, the Wildcats turned their underdog status into a positive. They fed off the notion that nobody expected them to make much noise against higher-ranked, more experienced teams, and never let the pressure of tournament play get to them.

"I think we went to the Final Four with an advantage," said Arizona guard Miles Simon. "We didn't have a care in the world. We weren't nervous out there."

After all, when you've lost four starters from last year's team, gone through the regular season with a 19-9 record and were barely a force to be reckoned with in your own conference, what's to be nervous about?

It helps to have a devil-may-care attitude when you find that you have to play three No. 1 seeds in a span of 11 days if you want to win the championship. And not only were they all No. 1 seeds; they were also the three winningest schools in college basketball history—Kentucky with 1,685 wins at the time, North Carolina with 1,675 and Kansas with 1,630.

Three times in recent years the Wildcats had been upset in the first round of NCAA tournament play, and it almost happened again. South Alabama led by 10 points with 7+ minutes remaining before Arizona went on a 12-0 run and pulled out a 65-57 victory. That was followed by a tight 73-69 victory over the College of Charleston.

Next up was Kansas, the top-ranked team in the nation and the No. 1 seed in the Southeast Regional. This time it was Arizona that got in front early, but the Wildcats' 13-point lead was slashed to one at one point, and they had to survive three potential game-tying shots before emerging with an 85-82 upset that left coach Lute Olson proclaiming, "We're not in awe of anybody. If they're going to beat us, they're going to have to do it on the court."

Arizona survived another comeback attempt in the regional final. Providence erased a 10-point deficit in the last 3:38 of regulation to tie the game, but the Wildcats won in overtime 96-92 to advance to the Final Four. There they defeated North Carolina, the top-seeded team in the East, 66-58, to advance to the championship game for the first time in school history.

The title game, a battle of Wildcats, was remarkably close, with 20 ties and 18 lead changes. It was Arizona's court quickness and skill from the foul line against Kentucky's three-point shooting ability, and Arizona won out by outscoring Kentucky 34-9 from the free-throw line.

"They have terrific guards," said Kentucky's Scott Padgett. "They did a great job penetrating, and that's what caused so many fouls."

Michael Bibby and Simon, the Arizona guards, used their quickness and passing ability to break Kentucky's full-court, man-to-man press. Bibby was particularly impressive as the primary ball handler, not wilting under the Kentucky pressure despite being just a freshman. Arizona led 33-32 at halftime and 44-38, before a 6-0 Kentucky run tied the score with 11:20 to play. That only set the stage for a frantic finish.

Kentucky's Wayne Turner missed a shot and then fouled out trying for an offensive rebound with 1:01 to play, and Bibby made both free throws to put Arizona in front 72-68. Kentucky's Ron Mercer nailed a three-pointer from the right side to cut the gap to one. Arizona, running out of a spread offense, stretched it to three when Bibby fed Bennett Davidson for a layup, but Kentucky's Anthony Epps responded with another three from nearly the same spot Mercer had shot his to send the game into overtime.

That's when Arizona won it from the foul line, scoring all 10 of its points in the five-minute extra period on free throws. Davidson sank a pair after 25 seconds to open the scoring, Kentucky missed its first three shots and was forced into fouling and never recovered. Four late free throws by Simon, the Final Four MVP who scored a game-high 30 points, clinched the victory.

"We just wanted it more," Simon said. "We wanted it more."

Simon and Bibby combined for 49 of Arizona's 84 points and took 30 of 58 field-goal attempts, proving too elusive to double-team in the open court.

"I love the way Arizona plays," said Kentucky coach Rick Pitino, whose team set a Final Four record by hoisting up 30 three-pointers. "They are no fluke. They got better and better. I love players who can pass, catch, dribble and shoot, and they have plenty of those guys."

For Olson, beaten in the Final Four three times, including twice with Arizona, the exciting victory left him drained. "I'm not sure two teams could expend more energy than these two teams did," he said. "For excitement, for effort, for tremendous defense, for the kind of game it was, I wish I could have been there as a spectator watching it. It seemed like it had everything that you could want in a game.

"I still have difficulty believing this happened," he added. "All I can say is, this is one tough group of young 'Cats."

00:48

. . . .

Boston's Comeback Kids

The rivalry between the Boston Celtics and Philadelphia 76ers, which peaked in the late 1960s when Bill Russell was leading the Celtics to eight consecutive championships until Wilt Chamberlain and the 76ers broke the string in 1967, was revived in the 1980s. For eight seasons, from 1980 through 1987, either Boston or Philadelphia represented the Eastern Conference in the NBA Finals against the best of the West, which usually was the Los Angeles Lakers of Kareem, Magic, Riles and Showtime.

Philadelphia, led by the brilliant Julius Erving, reached the NBA Finals three times in six years before finally winning the title in 1983. Boston, with Larry Bird, Kevin McHale and Robert Parish forming one of the best front lines ever, won three championships between 1981 and 1986 and made unsuccessful trips to the finals in 1985 and 1987.

Never was the Boston-Philly rivalry more intense than in 1981, when the Celtics forged one of the most remarkable repeated comebacks in basketball history. The Celtics would go on to beat Houston in six games for their 14th NBA title, but it was the series against Philadelphia that defined that team as a champion.

With their backs to the playoff wall, trailing three games to one in the best-of-seven Eastern Conference Finals, the Celtics erased second-half deficits not once, not twice, but three times, finally winning the series on Bird's 18-foot bank shot with 1:03 left that produced a 91-90 Game 7 victory.

"There was no one in the world I wanted to have the ball but me," Bird, in only his second pro season, said of his series-winning shot from the left of the lane. That self-confidence typified the Celtics' attitude. Even though they were facing elimination after losing three of four to an undeniably solid team that had matched Boston's 62-20 record during the regular season, the Celtics never panicked.

Team president Red Auerbach, the patriarch of the Celtics, wouldn't let them. M.L. Carr of the Celtics remembers the way Auerbach addressed the team:

"Red told us, 'Until they beat you one more time, they can't win a championship. They've got to beat you. And if you don't let 'em beat you one more time, you win it.' So we never thought of it that way—'Gee, we're down 3-1.' We thought, 'Red said they got to beat you one more time. Don't let 'em do it tonight.' You do that three times, you win it."

First, you have to do it once. And when Boston fell behind 59-49 at halftime of Game 5 on its home floor, the situation looked bleak. Even though Boston closed the gap in the second half, Philadelphia still seemed safe with a six-point lead and possession of the ball with 1:51 to play.

But a block by forward Cedric Maxwell set up a three-point play by point guard Tiny Archibald, slicing the lead in half. Philadelphia seemed shaken. A steal and basket by Bird drew Boston within one. The old Boston Garden on Causeway Street was rocking, and the Sixers were reeling. Another steal, by M.L. Carr, led to a pair of free throws and suddenly Boston was up by one. Another free throw by Carr closed out the scoring; Boston had tallied the final eight points of the game to win 111-109.

Stunned, the Sixers went home for Game 6 buoyed by the fact they had beaten Boston the last 11 times the teams had met in Philadelphia. But Game 6 at the Spectrum would not be No. 12, even though Philadelphia led by a dozen at halftime. Boston fought back behind the play of Maxwell, who had gotten involved in a fracas with fans under one of the baskets during the first half. Maxwell's two free throws iced the Celtics' 100-98 victory.

By now, Boston's spirit was soaring and Philadelphia had to be doubting itself. Yet when Game 7 started on May 3, 1981, it was the 76ers who grabbed the upper hand. Philadelphia led 31-26 after one quarter and 53-48 at halftime. For the third game in a row, the Celtics came out of the locker room following intermission, facing the challenge of trying to dig themselves out of a hole. And for the third game in a row, they did it.

They trailed 75-71 after three quarters, and with 4:34 remaining Philadelphia's lead was six points at 89-83. From that point on, buoyed by their noisy fans at Boston Garden, the Celtics put on the clamps. Philadelphia got the ball 10 times, but came away from those 10 possessions with just one point, a solitary free throw.

Referees Jake O'Donnell and Darell Garretson kept play stoppages to a minimum and allowed the players to decide the outcome. After the Celtics had tied the score at 89-89, Philadelphia center Darryl Dawkins wheeled to the basket and was stopped by three Boston defenders. No foul was called and Boston recovered the loose ball. "Players were knocking each other down all over the court. We were all beating each other to death," recalled Bird, who later called the game the most emotion-charged of his career.

While Boston's defense was stifling the Sixers, its offense managed to produce eight points—the final two when Bird brought the ball up the left side of the parquet floor, stopped at the foul line extended, then took a page from Hall of Famer Sam Jones' book by going glass for a bank shot and the game-winning basket. Philadelphia's Maurice Cheeks was fouled with 29 seconds left but made just one of two free throw attempts and Boston was able to hold on for a 91-90 win.

Basketball has seen many comebacks from greater deficits, but never has a team in such a pressure-packed situation put together three such comebacks against a quality opponent as did the Celtics, who won Games 5, 6 and 7 by a total of just five points.

"They had that mental toughness," said Philadelphia forward Bobby Jones. "We were up and I think we took things lightly. They kept at it and plugged away, and they made the breaks."

Not once, not twice, but three times.

00:47

· ·

San Antonio's Little General Comes Up Big

The 1999 San Antonio Spurs were led by a pair of 7-footers: the Admiral, David Robinson, and a young player so fundamentally sound, he defies nicknames, Tim Duncan. Avery Johnson was the Little General, the one who called the plays, set up the Texas Towers, directed traffic and made sure everything ran according to plan.

And every once in a while, he hit a jump shot—as he did with 47 seconds remaining in Game 5 of the 1999 NBA Finals, sinking an 18-footer from the left corner to nail down the Spurs' 78-77 victory over the New York Knicks and their first NBA championship.

Johnson is one of the most popular players in the league, among his peers as well as the media who voted him the 1998 NBA Sportsmanship Award and a place on the 1999 All-Interview team. His championship ring did not come easily. That only made it that much more precious.

Unlike Duncan and Robinson, who entered the NBA as No. 1 overall draft picks, or Spurs forward Sean Elliott, who came in as a Wooden Award-winner and two-time All-American, Johnson came into the league as an unknown commodity. Although he averaged 13.3 assists per game as a senior at Southern University, Johnson was not selected in the 1988 NBA Draft and had to play in the summer USBL just to earn a free-agent tryout with the Seattle SuperSonics. Over the next six years he was traded by Seattle and waived by Denver, Houston and San Antonio. Even after rejoining the Spurs, starting at point guard in 1992-93 and averaging a team-high 7.5 assists per game, Johnson's status was so shaky, he felt he had to sign a one-year contract with the Golden State Warriors before going back to the Spurs for good on July 21, 1994.

Despite averaging at least 10 points and seven assists per game for five consecutive seasons, Johnson could never silence his legion of doubters. At 5-feet-11 he was too small, they said, making it all too easy for opponents to shoot over him. His jump shot supposedly wasn't reliable enough to take the pressure off San Antonio's big men—when playing the Spurs, many teams had their point guard lay off Johnson and double-team Duncan and/or Robinson, daring Johnson to beat them with the outside shot. Even during the midst of the Spurs' marvelous run in 1999, guard Damon Stoudamire of the Portland Trail Blazers was widely quoted as saying that no team with Avery Johnson as its point guard would ever win an NBA title —a quote Stoudamire retracted shortly before the Spurs won their crown.

Yet in the title-clinching game, it was Johnson who not only orchestrated the San Antonio offense but hit the game-winning shot. "Mario said, 'Shoot it,' and I listen to him," said Johnson, joking with teammate Mario Elie, who won two titles with Houston and added a measure of toughness and exuberance upon joining the Spurs.

"I'm so happy for Avery because, first of all, he's worked so hard during his career," said veteran guard Steve Kerr. "And I'm happy because it was a jump shot. Everybody says that the guy can't shoot. They've been saying it for years, and he's worked on that thing so hard that to win a championship with a jump shot for him is a perfect microcosm of his career."

"Little Big Man hits the J," crowed Jaren Jackson, another Spurs reserve guard. "It was a dagger. They've been killing him all his career about that jumper. Sting 'em, A.J., sting 'em!"

The New York Knicks, with center Patrick Ewing sidelined by a torn Achilles tendon, were no match for the Spurs' two 7-footers at either end of the floor. Duncan was the Most Valuable Player of the Finals, averaging 27.4 points and 14.0 rebounds per game, shooting 54 percent from the field and teaming with Robinson to prevent the Knicks from getting much of anything inside. New York, forced to rely on big guards Allan Houston and Latrell Sprewell for their offense, shot just 39.2 percent for the series.

While Duncan got the headlines for his excellence and Robinson for sacrificing his individual stats for the good of the team, the rest of the Spurs played their roles to perfection. Elie came in and provided toughness and an outside shooting touch, while Jackson and Kerr were three-point threats off the bench. Elliott was a double-figure scorer driving to the basket and shooting from outside, and his defense was an unheralded asset for the Spurs. Malik Rose gave San Antonio muscle off the bench, enabling coach Gregg Popovich to give Duncan and especially Robinson whatever rest they needed.

And Johnson orchestrated the performance, making sure Duncan and Robinson got the ball in the half-court offense, keeping the other players involved, running the fast break when the opportunity was there and hitting the timely jumper. Johnson averaged 9.2 points and 7.2 assists and shot 50 percent from the field in the finals.

While Duncan (31 points) and Sprewell (35) were the big scorers in Game 5 of the series, when the Knicks left Johnson alone in the final minute, he made them pay. New York led 77-75 with 3:12 to play but would not score after that. Duncan's free throw with 2:33 left cut the lead to one, and on the game-winning play, the Knicks were so concerned about the inside presence of the Towers that Johnson was able to spot up in the left corner, catch and shoot without much pressure.

"On that particular play, I was open and felt good about it. That's my shot, I love corner shots," said Johnson, who pointed to a conversation he had with Kerr over the summer as helping him approach his shooting with greater confidence. Before joining the Spurs in the summer of 1998, Kerr earned three championship rings with the Chicago Bulls as a spot-up shooter alongside Michael Jordan and Scottie Pippen.

Johnson said, "Kerr told me, 'The main thing is, you have to know you're going to shoot it. Don't hesitate. Shoot it. Let it go. And get to the spots where you like to operate.' I got right there within 18 feet, which is where I like to operate, and it felt good."

Then Johnson, sitting on stage in the media interview room after Game 5, thought back on his twisting journey from an undrafted collegian in 1988 to an NBA champion in 1999.

"My whole life," said Johnson, "not just on the basketball court but off the court, is a big example to a lot of people out there —a lot of kids especially, but also a lot of adults—that need to persevere in their own situations. It's been an example of just not really giving up, just hanging in there when you get cut on Christmas Eve, when the Spurs cut you on David Robinson's wedding day after you were in the wedding.

"It's just unbelievable that I'm sitting up here talking to you guys. I don't know what to say."

00:46

. . . .

Wilt Scores 100!

Wilt Chamberlain always seemed larger than life, an athlete of Bunyanesque stature who overshadowed nearly all around him. He was the most dominating offensive force the game of basketball has ever seen, and on March 2, 1962, he turned in a most remarkable performance.

Playing against the New York Knicks before a sparse gathering of 4,124 in the Hershey Arena, where the Philadelphia Warriors played a few of their home games in the early '60s in an effort to draw fans from outside the city, Chamberlain scored an even 100 points in a 169-147 Philadelphia victory. Not 98 points, not 102, but a nice, round 100—an imposing record by a most imposing player.

"It is a mythic game because Wilt scored exactly 100, no more, no less," said Harvey Pollack, who was in charge of publicity and statistics for Philadelphia and who covered the game for the Associated Press, United Press International and the *Philadelphia Inquirer,* none of which sent reporters.

Chamberlain likes to speak of how the game is shrouded in mystery, since it was not televised and no videotape exists. "People have been able to embellish it without facts getting in the way," he said with a smile. "Over the years the memories get better. It's like your first girlfriend—the picture you have in your head is always better than how she looked in real life."

Standing 7-foot-1 and weighing a muscular 275 pounds, with the speed, quickness and agility of the track-and-field star he had been in high school, Chamberlain was unstoppable on his way to the basket, whether leaning in for a finger-roll or turning for a hook shot or jumper. Yet he chose to downplay his power game and took pride in developing the all-around shooting and ballhandling skills of players half a foot shorter.

"The assumption was that I scored more than anyone else because I was bigger than everyone else," he said. "But I wasn't that much bigger. Centers such as Charlie Share and Clyde Lovellette weighed more than I did. Walter Dukes was just as tall as I am. But everyone said my success was due to my size, and that's a real kick. When I was a kid, I worked at the game five, six, seven hours a day. I studied the game, learned how to pass, to rebound, to play defense."

He also was immensely strong, although he always kept his temper in check. "I developed my own weight program before any other basketball player even thought about it," Chamberlain said with pride. "I was stronger than everyone else because I made myself stronger. I built up my body."

How strong was he? "Once Wilt got upset with me and dunked the ball so hard that it went through the rim with such force that it broke my toe as it hit the floor," said rival center Johnny Kerr. And don't think he was exaggerating, because Philadelphia's Billy Cunningham vouches for him. "Johnny was embarrassed to let everyone know that he got a broken toe from one of Wilt's dunks, so he went down to the other end of the court, acted as if he tripped, grabbed his foot and went out of the game," said Cunningham, who played both with and against Chamberlain.

Chamberlain certainly was unstoppable that night in Hershey, Pennsylvania. The Knicks' starting center, Phil Jordan, was suffering from the flu and did not make the bus ride down from New York, and while it's questionable how much of a difference he would have made, his replacements, Darrall Imhoff and Cleveland Buckner, were helpless in trying to contain Chamberlain. He scored 23 points in the first quarter and had 41 by halftime, then tacked on 28 in the third quarter as the fans began to chant, "Give It to Wilt! Give It to Wilt!"

That's exactly what the Warriors did, feeding Chamberlain at every opportunity in the fourth quarter. The Knicks tried fouling other Philadelphia players to keep the ball away from Chamberlain, but the Warriors countered by committing fouls of their own to get the ball back.

"The game was a real pain in the neck to call," said Pete D'Ambrosio, who refereed the game along with Willie Smith. "The last three minutes of game time took about 20 minutes. The Knicks were jumping on guys just to keep the ball away from Wilt. Then New York would get the ball, and Philly would foul."

"When we got the ball, they were fouling everyone except Wilt so he wouldn't get 100," recalled Philadelphia forward Tom Meschery. "So we would take the ball out of bounds and throw high lobs directly to Wilt near the basket. When Wilt wanted the ball, he was big enough and strong enough to go get it. Guys were hanging on his back and he was still catching the pass and scoring."

Chamberlain got up to 98 points with 1:19 to go in the game, then Philadelphia got the ball back and Chamberlain took a shot that missed. Joe Ruklick grabbed the offensive rebound and fed it back to Chamberlain, who laid it in with 46 seconds left to give him 100 points. Fans raced onto the court and play was halted as Chamberlain went to the locker room, where PR man Pollack scrawled "100" on a piece of paper and had Chamberlain hold it up for photographers.

In erasing his own NBA single-game scoring record of 78 points set earlier that season, Chamberlain shot 36-for-63 from the field and 28-for-32 from the foul line. The latter is remarkable, as Chamberlain was a notoriously weak free-throw shooter, connecting on just .511 from the line for his career.

Chamberlain went on to average an NBA-record 50.4 points per game in that 1961-62 season, when he totaled 4,029 points and became the only player to surpass 4,000 points in one season. What's more, he also led the league in rebounding with 25.7 rpg and was second in field-goal percentage at .506.

In another remarkable achievement, Chamberlain averaged 48.5 minutes per game—an amazing feat when you remember that a regulation NBA game lasts only 48 minutes. Seven of Philadelphia's games went into overtime that season and the Warriors played a total of 10 extra five-minute periods. Chamberlain was on the court for 3,882 of a possible 3,890 minutes, going the full distance in 79 of the team's 80 games.

But the record that captured fans' imagination and has grown in stature over the years beyond all others, is the 100-point game. Even Chamberlain, who downplayed the feat as "inevitable" when it first happened because he was scoring so prolifically every night, has come to appreciate it and embrace it.

"As time goes by," he reflected more than three decades later, "I feel more and more a part of that 100-point game. It has become my handle, and I've come to realize just what I did."

While no videotape of the game exists, an audiotape was found more than 30 years after the event, and it revealed an interesting postscript. Fans had stormed onto the court after Chamberlain reached the century mark, halting play with Philadelphia in front 169-147. While Pollack was posing Chamberlain with his "100" sign in the locker room, the officials actually cleared the court, play resumed and the final 46 seconds were run off the clock. But since Pollack was the game's official scorer, and he had the scorebook with him, those 46 seconds never were officially recorded. So as far as the NBA is concerned, it's as if they never were played.

00:45

• •

Spanich Makes Use of Ultra-Green Light

Southern Cal coach Henry Bibby figures when you've got a shooter on your team, let him shoot. That's why he gave Adam Spanich what he calls the "ultra-green light," which means, "go and don't even think about stopping."

"That is Adam's job," said Bibby of the 6-foot-7 forward. "We want him to shoot the ball. He is one of the best shooters I have ever been around. He can flat-out shoot the basketball."

Spanich made the most of his opportunity on January 17, 1999, against the University of Oregon. He scored 26 points and shot 6-for-7 from three-point range as the Trojans defeated the Ducks 85-84. But that's the least of it.

Incredibly, Spanich sank not one but two of his three-point field goals in the last eight-tenths of a second, personally erasing a five-point deficit and giving Southern Cal the road win.

"It was heaven-sent," said Bibby. "It's not supposed to fall into place like that. Everything happened our way."

"You can't describe a feeling like that," said Oregon point guard Darius Wright. "It's like riding a roller coaster. Your guts fall out."

Oregon was riding high for most of the game. The Ducks led 46-34 at halftime and were ahead 58-42 five minutes into the second period. Three turnovers in the next 2+ minutes allowed Southern Cal to cut into the deficit, but a trio of three-pointers by reserve Terik Brown put Oregon in front by a seemingly comfortable 71-56 margin with 8:17 to play.

That's when the roller-coaster car crested, and it was all downhill for the Ducks after that.

"The game was lost on mental toughness," said Oregon coach Ernie Kent. "In the last 10 or 12 minutes, where we had opportunities to take care of the ball, get on the boards and put free throws in, we didn't do it."

Spanich came off the bench to score 16 of his 26 points in the second half. Guard Elias Ayuso supported him with five three-pointers as USC shot 12-for-19 from behind the arc. "That was our plan —shoot the three every time down, because we couldn't penetrate on them," said Bibby.

The Trojans shot 61 percent from the field in the second half and 53 percent overall, and outbounded Oregon 35-25 for the game. But none of that would have mattered if Oregon had made its free throws down the stretch and been more careful with the ball.

"We didn't put them away," said Wright. "If we had made our free throws, the game wouldn't even have been close."

As Southern Cal was coming back, Oregon missed 7 of 11 free throws in the final four minutes. After a basket by Oregon's A.D. Smith made it 81-74 with 1:54 left, the Ducks missed 6 of 9 from the line but still led 84-79 with nine seconds to play.

Jeff Trepagnier missed a shot for Southern Cal, but as the two teams scrambled for the rebound, the ball went out of bounds and the Trojans retained possession, courtesy of the alternating possession arrow. With 2.8 seconds showing on the clock, Oregon called a timeout to get itself settled on defense; the move was a questionable one, since it allowed USC (which was out of timeouts) to map out a three-point play off the inbounds pass.

Spanich caught the pass in the right corner and lofted a three-pointer that went through the net with :00.8 on the game clock. Smith then attempted to end the game by throwing his inbounds pass deep, but he didn't throw it deep enough. Spanich, anticipating the play, broke back toward mid-court right after he released his shot, picked off the inbounds pass just short of mid-court and immediately fired a prayer that was answered at the buzzer. Oregon argued that the inbounds pass was tipped by the player guarding Smith on the baseline and the clock should have started then, which means time would have run out before the ball even reached Spanich, but to no avail.

"I can't worry about whether the call was good or not," said Kent. "The kid made a great play and it shouldn't have come to that. That probably won't happen again in college basketball this year, but it happened to us tonight."

"I just didn't throw the pass deep enough," said Smith, shouldering the blame. "I threw it where their best three-point shooter could get it. That's a personal mistake that cost us a big game."

"I thought it was going to be right on," Spanich said of his final shot. "But I thought it might be a little short, it might hit the rim. I didn't think it would go right in."

"It was a great shot," said Oregon's Wright. "When he let it go, I said, 'Please, don't go in.' But it was all net."

"I've probably coached 800 games, and that may be the best shot I've ever seen," said Bibby.

00:44

• •

Jerry West: "Mr. Clutch"

Jerry West was tagged with the nickname "Zeke from Cabin Creek" by teammate Elgin Baylor when he joined the Los Angeles Lakers in 1960. Baylor liked to call all country folk Zeke, and since Cheylan, West Virginia, where West grew up, didn't exactly have a ring to it, he turned to the nearby town of Cabin Creek and came up with the nickname.

Over the course of his brilliant 14-year pro career, all spent with the Lakers, West would earn another, more appropriate, nickname: "Mr. Clutch."

West was a 6-foot-2 guard who could do it all. He averaged 27.0 points, 6.7 assists and 5.8 rebounds per game as a pro and led the Lakers to the playoffs 13 times in 14 seasons. He never won Most Valuable Player honors, as his career spanned those of Bill Russell, Wilt Chamberlain and Oscar Robertson, among other superstars, but he was the MVP of the 1972 All-Star Game and the 1969 NBA Finals—the only player from a losing team ever to be voted Finals MVP. In 1965, in a six-game playoff series against the Baltimore Bullets, West averaged 46.3 points per game, a record that has withstood the assaults of all, including Michael Jordan.

West, like Robertson, his teammate on the powerful U.S. Olympic team that won a gold medal in Rome in 1960, defied pigeonholing into the current terms point guard or shooting guard. He filled both roles brilliantly, scoring by slashing to the basket or hitting his picture-perfect jump shot, dribbling and passing to deftly set up his teammates, running an offense with aplomb. In 1970 he led the NBA in scoring; two years later he topped the league in assists.

Highly competitive, West was a perfectionist who demanded the best from himself as well as those around him, another trait he shared with Robertson. That drove him to make the most of his ability as a player and served him well in his behind-the-scenes work as the Lakers' general manager and head of basketball operations, but it hurt him in his three seasons as coach of the Lakers in the late '70s. While Los Angeles had a winning record each season, it never won an NBA title and West simmered when he felt his players weren't living up to their abilities or weren't taking the game as seriously as he did.

"He took a loss harder than any player I've ever known," said longtime Lakers broadcaster Chick Hearn. "He would sit by himself and stare into space. A loss just ripped his guts out."

"He was the greatest competitor I've ever seen," said Hot Rod Hundley, a Laker teammate whose scoring records West broke at

West Virginia. "I don't care what you're playing, he wants to win. His nickname was 'Mr. Clutch' and he carried that moniker well, because every time we were in that situation, boom, he'd make that shot."

Nonetheless, some of West's greatest performances came in defeat, and he knew more than his share of frustration in his playing career. Nine times the Lakers reached the NBA Finals with West in the lineup; eight times they came up on the short end, losing to Boston six times and New York twice. Only in 1972, when the Lakers—who had set a record by winning 33 games in a row during the regular season—beat the Knicks in five games, did West win a championship.

Particularly frustrating were the 1969 Finals against Boston, when the Lakers lost Game 7 at home 108-106 despite 42 points, 13 rebounds and 12 assists by West in one of the greatest playoff performances ever. It earned him the Finals MVP and tributes from the Celtics, many of whom went to the Laker locker room after the game for some consoling words. "Jerry, I love you," John Havlicek told an inconsolable West. "He is the master," said Celtics guard Larry Siegfried. "They can talk about the others, build them up, but he is the one. He is the only guard."

The 1970 NBA Finals are best known for Willis Reed's inspirational march onto the floor at Madison Square Garden moments before Game 7, when the hobbled Reed scored New York's first two baskets and sparked the Knicks to a 113-99 victory over the Lakers.

But Game 3 of that series produced another memorable moment in NBA history, courtesy of "Mr. Clutch."

With the series tied at 1-1, the Knicks had erased a 14-point halftime deficit in Game 3 and taken a 102-100 lead on a bucket by Dave DeBusschere with three seconds to play. The Lakers were out of timeouts, so West took the inbounds pass from Chamberlain in the backcourt, dribbled as far as he dared and then launched a 60-

footer. It found its target as DeBusschere, under the basket, threw his arms up in disgust.

Today, that shot would have given the Lakers a 103-102 victory. But there was no three-point field goal in those days, and so it only tied the score and sent the game into overtime. The Knicks managed to regroup for a 111-108 win and went on to take the series, relegating West's remarkable basket to a historical footnote.

Another memorable basket by West came at the end of the 1972 All-Star Game, and anyone who saw that game will never forget it. With the score tied at 110-110 and nine seconds remaining, West took an inbounds pass from Robertson and brought the ball over the mid-court line against Walt Frazier—one of the game's greatest scorers against one of its top defenders, one-on-one, me-against-you, stop me if you can.

West dribbled the ball up the left sideline, then switched his dribble to his right hand as he cut back toward the middle. Robertson set a pick near the foul line, but Frazier saw it and stayed between the two offensive players as West neared the top of the key. With time running down, West stopped, squared to the basket and launched his jumper from the top of the key just a shade quicker than Frazier could react for the block.

As soon as the ball was released, Bill Russell, doing the network television commentary, said, "Two points." Sure enough, it sailed through—nothing but net—with one second left. "You could see that coming," added Russell. "You know he's going to get two. You can anticipate that going in. You could see it in the backcourt."

And it's because of shots like that, West was nicknamed "Mr. Clutch."

00:43

. . . .

Celtics Win First Title, but Just Barely

Imagine a team winning Game 7 of the NBA Finals with a starting backcourt that shoots 5-for-40 from the field, a rousing .125 mark. It's possible, especially when two rookie frontcourt men on that same team combine for 56 points and 55 rebounds in that game.

To win their first NBA championship, the 1957 Boston Celtics needed brilliant performances by forward Tom Heinsohn and center Bill Russell, the aforementioned rookies, to offset the poor shooting of veteran guards Bob Cousy and Bill Sharman and win Game 7 of the NBA Finals, a game in which the St. Louis Hawks barely misconnected on one of the most audacious game-ending plays in basketball annals.

It was a remarkable finish to a remarkable game, and the best place to start a recounting of what happened is from the finish.

With two seconds left in the second overtime, Jim Loscutoff, the Celtics' bruising forward, was fouled by Ed Macauley. Loscutoff sank both free throws to give Boston a 125-123 lead and the Hawks called a timeout. St. Louis needed to go the length of the floor for a chance to tie, since the NBA did not yet have the rule under which a team can move the ball up to mid-court with a timeout.

Most teams will attempt to have a player throw a long pass to a teammate, who will try to come to the ball, catch it, turn and shoot before time runs out, as Duke did to beat Kentucky in the famous play from the 1992 NCAA Tournament. That's the play everyone expects, however, so defenders invariably circle in front of their men and knock the pass away as time expires.

Expecting that Boston would do this, Alex Hannum, the Hall of Famer who was player-coach of the Hawks, came up with a different idea. If the defender is going to come forward in between the passer and the target, why not throw it over his head so the offensive player can catch it while facing the basket and get off a quick shot? Since an 85-foot lob pass seemed doomed to failure, Hannum came up with the idea of tossing a pass off the backboard so that teammate Bob Pettit could grab the carom and attempt the shot.

Macauley remembers Hannum telling his players what he wanted: "Alex said, 'I'm going to throw the ball the length of the court. It's going to hit the backboard. Then, Pettit, you'll get the rebound and tip it in.' There were nine guys around Hannum and we all were nodding like we knew what he was talking about. But I was like everyone else. I was thinking that Alex had a hard time hitting the backboard from 15 feet, so how was he going to do it from 94 feet?"

"I kept thinking I'd never heard anything like it before," echoed Pettit. "And Alex was so sure of himself. He looked right at me and said, 'Pettit, you'll get the rebound and tip it in.'"

"It was a gamble," conceded Hannum, "but Pettit was the greatest offensive rebounder I'd ever seen. I figured if I could get the ball on the board, we had a chance."

As expected, Boston's defenders played the passing lanes, getting between their men and Hannum. So he took the ball beyond the end line and fired it the length of the court, and to the astonishment of the crowd at Boston Garden, to say nothing of the Celtic players, he hit the opposite backboard 94 feet away. What's more, the carom came toward Pettit, St. Louis' leading scorer, who had been the league's MVP a year earlier.

That's where the Hawks' luck ran out. Pettit grabbed the ball but hurried his shot in order to get it off in time. It rolled off the rim, and Boston had its victory and first-ever championship.

"I caught the ball in midair and shot it before I came down," said Pettit. "The ball rolled around the rim and came out. Really, as crazy as it sounds, I should have made the shot. Alex's pass was perfect."

Cousy called that championship the most satisfying of his career, and Russell still chooses to wear the ring he received after that season from among the 11 he earned. "The first one is always the hardest, and it's also the most satisfying," said Celtics coach Red Auerbach. "Everywhere I went that following summer, I could tell myself, 'I'm the coach of the world champions.'"

The amazing finish capped a series in which two games went to double overtime, and four of the seven games were decided by a margin of two points apiece.

The Celtics were favored after winning the East Division with a 44-28 record, compared with St. Louis' 34-38 mark, enough for a three-way tie for the top spot in a West Division in which all four clubs had losing records. Cousy led the league in assists and earned MVP honors, Heinsohn was Rookie of the Year, Sharman made All-NBA First Team and Russell brought it all together after joining the club in December following the completion of the Olympics in Melbourne, Australia. With 48 regular-season games in which to adjust to his new teammates, plus a three-game sweep of Syracuse in the playoffs, Russell was fresh for the finals.

It didn't take St. Louis long to dispel any notion of a lopsided series. With the magnificent Pettit scoring 37 points and Ed Macauley and Slater Martin getting 23 apiece, the Hawks stunned the Celtics at Boston Garden 125-123 in double overtime on a long basket by Jack Coleman that just beat the 24-second shot clock in the closing seconds.

Auerbach adjusted his defense to contain Pettit in Game 2 and Boston limited the 6-foot-9 forward to 11 points in a 119-99 rout that tied the series. When the scene shifted to St. Louis, defense dominated Game 3, but Pettit rose to the occasion with a long shot that gave the Hawks a 100-98 win. Again, Boston bounced back, beating the Hawks 123-118 in St. Louis to draw even, then taking Game 5 at home 124-109 behind Cousy's 31 points to go up 3-2. But the Celtics couldn't close it out, losing another defensive struggle 96-94 in Game 6 in St. Louis. Cousy opened the door when he missed from the foul line with 12 seconds left and the score tied, and rookie Cliff Hagan led St. Louis through by tipping home Pettit's desperation shot at the buzzer.

So it was on to Boston Garden for Game 7, which was nationally televised (a rarity in those days) and turned out to be so exciting, it helped cement the NBA's place on the American sports scene. Although Cousy shot 2-for-20 and Sharman 3-for-20, Heinsohn and Russell made up for their lack of production, Heinsohn getting 37 points and 23 rebounds and Russell 19 points and 32 rebounds, plus five blocks—one of which would prove crucial.

St. Louis led by four points with two minutes to go, but three free throws by Boston cut the lead to one. Coleman got ahead of the field and was headed in for a layup, but Russell put on a burst of speed, caught up and blocked the shot at the last moment. Russell would revolutionize the game with his defensive prowess, and this was an early example.

"The greatest play I ever saw in basketball," said Heinsohn more than three decades later, "was Russell blocking Coleman's shot. He went by me like I was standing still, and I was near mid-court. He was the fastest man on the team."

Russell went on to score a basket on the ensuing possession, but Cousy could hit only one of two free throws to make it 103-101 and leave the door open for the Hawks. Pettit, who averaged 29.8 points and 16.8 rebounds per game in the series and came up big with 39 points and 19 rebounds in Game 7, sent it into overtime by sinking two free throws in the closing seconds of regulation.

Boston had St. Louis on the ropes in the five-minute extra period, but a jumper by Coleman, who had hit the game-winner in the series opener, sent it to a second overtime period tied at 113-113. That's when Boston outscored St. Louis 12-10, thanks to Loscutoff's late free throws, and survived Hannum's stratagem as Pettit's shot fell off the rim.

The Celtics had their first taste of victory, one they found to their liking. "We've been trying to get to the top for seven years and now we're finally here," said Cousy. "People are calling us great, but now we've got to do it again, just to show that we're the greatest." Although the Celtics wouldn't win the title again the next season, they would go on to win 11 championships in the 13-year period from 1956-57 through 1968-69, the greatest dynasty in major American professional sports history.

00:42

. . . .

Bob Pettit's Revenge

"In his day, Bob Pettit was the best power forward there was," said Red Auerbach, the Boston Celtics' patriarch who coached against Pettit in four championship series between 1957 and 1961. "Elgin Baylor was a close second. Pettit could do more things than Baylor, because he could play some center. And he was a better rebounder than Baylor.

"Pettit was Mr. Clean, Mr. All-America. He was like John Havlicek, a clean liver, just a super guy, but very, very competitive. He would play all out, whether he was 50 points ahead or 50 behind. It didn't matter. That's the only way he knew how to play — all out."

Pettit, the St. Louis Hawks' superstar forward who played in the All-Star Game in each of his 11 seasons in the NBA, didn't have to wait long to make up for missing the last shot of the 1957 NBA Finals, which would have sent Game 7 into a third overtime but instead let Boston win 125-123 in double OT for the championship. The teams met again for the title the following year, and this time Pettit was not to be denied.

Pettit averaged 24.6 points and 17.4 rebounds in leading the Hawks to a 41-31 record and the 1957-58 Western Division title, and also earned MVP honors in the All-Star Game with a 28-point, 24-rebound performance. In addition, the Hawks had solid pros like Slater Martin and Jack McMahon at guard and Cliff Hagan,

Ed Macauley, Chuck Share and Jack Coleman in the frontcourt. They were coached by Alex Hannum, who had taken over as a player-coach midway through the previous season but retired as a player to devote full attention to his bench duties.

The Celtics, meanwhile, were riding the high of their first NBA championship the previous spring to a league-best 49-23 record. Bill Sharman led the team in scoring at 22.3 points per game, Bill Russell led the entire NBA in rebounding at 22.7 per game and Bob Cousy led the league in assists at 7.1 per game.

Boston was favored, but St. Louis stunned the Celtics by winning the opening game of the series at Boston Garden 104-102. Boston came back to win Game 2 in a blowout 136-112.

Game 3 in St. Louis's Kiel Auditorium turned out to be calamitous for the Celtics. Not only did they lose the game 111-108, but Russell suffered a sprained ankle in the third minute of play while blocking a shot by Pettit—and was called for goaltending on the play to boot. The injury would sideline the Celtics center for the next two games, and he could only play 20 minutes at half-speed in Game 6.

The 6-foot-9 Russell, voted by his peers the league's Most Valuable Player in only his second pro season, was vital to Boston's game both for his rebounding and for his shot-blocking presence. Without Russell lurking in the lane as the anchor of the team's defense, or with him at less than 100 percent, the Hawks felt freer to attack the hoop and drive for layups.

The loss of Russell was compounded by the absence of "Jungle" Jim Loscutoff, the Celtics' 6-foot-5, 230-pound enforcer, who missed all but five games of the season due to injury. That left 6-7 second-year man Tom Heinsohn, 6-7 Jack Nichols and 6-9 Arnie Risen to contend with Pettit and the rest of the Hawks' talented frontcourt. It was not an ideal situation—Heinsohn was better known for his scoring (he picked up the nickname "Ack-Ack" because he could put up shots with machine-gun-like rapidity) than his defense,

Nichols was a journeyman playing for his fourth NBA team and Risen, a three-time All-Star, was 33 and in the final season of his fine 13-year pro career.

Nevertheless, the Celtics managed to circle the wagons and post a 109-98 victory in St. Louis to even the series at two victories apiece. The Hawks, however, went into Boston Garden and came away with a 102-100 win in Game 5, giving them an opportunity to wrap up the title on their home floor. They had let it get away the previous year, failing to hold a four-point lead in the final two minutes of Game 7; they were not about to let it happen again.

Pettit was never better than in Game 6. He scored 31 points in the first three quarters of the game at Kiel Auditorium, then personally took command by scoring 19 of his team's final 21 points for a total of 50. His last two points came on a jumper with 15 seconds remaining and gave the Hawks a 110-107 lead, more than enough to withstand one last Celtic basket and come away with a 110-109 victory and the franchise's only NBA championship.

Russell, hobbled for the finale, was no match for Pettit, and neither were Boston's other frontcourt men. His combination of skill and determination made Pettit a Hall of Famer and the first player in NBA history to score 20,000 career points. "Bob made 'second effort' a part of the sport's vocabulary," said Russell. "He kept coming at you more than any man in the game. He was always battling for position, fighting you off the boards."

"I was an old-timer when he was a rookie, and I saw him mature into a great player," said Hannum, who briefly played with Pettit at the end of his own career before becoming his coach. "He's a winner, whether it was in playing cards or on the court. I always said it was no fun to play poker against Bob Pettit, because he always played to win, not just to have fun."

The 50 points by Pettit matched the record for an NBA Playoff game set by Bob Cousy of Boston against Syracuse in 1953. Cousy, however, had the benefit of a four-overtime game, and one that was so marred by fouls that 30 of his points came from the free-throw line (as opposed to 12 by Pettit). Pettit had 19 field goals (in 34 attempts), to just 10 field goals by Cousy.

It also broke the record for an NBA Finals game, held by George Mikan of Minneapolis, who scored 42 points against Washington in 1949. Michael Jordan now holds the record for points in a playoff game with 63 (Chicago at Boston, April 20, 1986), and Elgin Baylor holds the mark for points in a finals game with 61 (Los Angeles at Boston, April 14, 1962).

In the minds of the Celtics and their fans, the injury to Russell was a mitigating factor in Boston's inability to repeat.

"Everyone knows how great Russell was and what he meant to us, and he was severely hampered by that ankle," said Cousy. "All I know is that without question, the Hawks were the second-best team that year."

"It is senseless to ask, 'What if?'" countered Hagan. "You only know for sure what actually happened, and in 1958 Russell was on the court and we beat his team in six games."

"I take nothing away from St. Louis," said Auerbach. "You could see it wasn't the same Russell, and we almost won anyway. You can always look for excuses. We just got beat."

"We won that title because Bobby Pettit would not let us lose," said Share. "He had 50 points, and nothing the Celtics can say can take that away from Pettit."

00:41

The Real-Life Hoosiers: Milan High School

When it was released in 1986, the movie *Hoosiers* touched a responsive chord in millions of viewers, many of whom were relative strangers to the sport of basketball. The story of dedication and sacrifice and teamwork extolled values that are cherished by sports fans and non-sports fans alike.

It also made national celebrities out of Marvin Wood and Bobby Plump, the coach of the real-life team on which the movie was based and the player from that team who scored the game-winning basket, just like on screen.

Milan 32, Muncie Central 30. It's one of the most revered scores in the history of Indiana state high school basketball, and Indiana is one state where they truly revere their high school basketball history.

"Now that I look back on it, I'm not so sure it wasn't destiny," said Wood, who coached for two years at Milan before moving on to several other schools in the state.

It was a triumph of David over Goliath. Unlike most states, where schools are grouped into different classifications based on enrollment and compete against other schools of roughly the same size, Indiana—until a controversial change to a one-class system in 1996-97—held just one state tournament for all schools, big or small. That way, even the smallest school could dream of going to Indianapolis, winning the state championship and being crowned the best basketball team in the entire state, not just in its own class.

Wood, who was 26 when Milan won the state crown in 1954, preached a patient offense based on passing and teamwork and holding the ball for a good shot, as well as a trapping zone-press defense to force turnovers. "Woody was a coach ahead of his time, at least in Southeastern Indiana," said Plump. "He brought a disciplined offense to our part of the state, which up to that time had been schooled mainly on freelance basketball."

But when Wood came to Milan High School, with a student body of 161, he knew that the best chance for upsetting bigger schools was to dictate the tempo of the game and make the opponent play your style of ball. That formula helped Milan advance to the tournament semifinals in 1953 before bowing to South Bend Central, the eventual champion, so its march to the title in 1954 wasn't a total surprise, but it was remarkable nonetheless.

After winning its three games in the sectional and the first in the regional, Milan went up against a bigger and more athletic team from Crispus Attucks of Indianapolis (including a sophomore by the name of Oscar Robertson) in the regional final.

"When we played Crispus Attucks, I know they felt we were going to hold the ball right away," said Wood, who had enough confidence in his team to try a different tactic. "We're going to see what we can do with our regular style," he told his players. "If it doesn't work, then we'll have to change gears."

Milan defeated Crispus Attucks 65-52, handing Robertson his only defeat in 28 state tournament games, to earn a berth in the Final Four in Indianapolis.

Milan defeated Terre Haute Gerstmeyer 60-48 in the semifinals, but Bob Engel, one of the team's biggest and best players, suffered a back injury. Wood knew that more than ever he'd have to control the pace in the final against Muncie Central, a school that had won eight state titles and been to the Final Four 17 times. Muncie's frontcourt players stood 6-5, 6-4 and 6-2; Milan's tallest player, Ron Truitt, was 6-2, but its center, Gene White, was just 5-11.

Wood went to his "cat-and-mouse" game, in which Plump was stationed above the top of the circle, almost at the mid-court line, while two teammates stood on the wings parallel to the foul line and two others stood at the baseline in the corners. This spread the defenders, the objective being to create enough room for Plump or Ray Craft to drive the middle and then shoot or pass off to a teammate.

Milan jumped ahead early with its deliberate offense and led 25-17 at the half, but Muncie gradually wore down its smaller opponent and moved in front 28-26 by holding Milan without a basket in the third quarter. Wood wasn't about to panic, but he also knew he had to work the clock because the more the teams were out on the floor, the more the advantage seemed to be swinging toward Muncie.

"We felt if we could hang in there toward the end of the game, our experience would finally pay off," said Wood. So he decided to take the air out of the ball, even though his team was down by two. Plump held the ball for 4 minutes, 14 seconds, to the amazement of the crowd at Butler Fieldhouse.

"Everybody was going crazy wondering what the hell was going on out there," said Plump. "We're behind in the tournament and yet we're holding the ball. I looked over at Coach Wood, and he's just sitting there nonchalantly."

"I felt, hey, we have to do everything we can to conserve what energy we have to give us a chance at the end of the game," said Wood. "So we slowed it down earlier than we ever had."

Wood, who later told writers he was trying to think of something to do while Plump was standing there holding the ball, called a timeout with a little over three minutes left and brought his team out of the stall. Plump missed a jumper, but Muncie turned the ball over against the press and Craft tied the game with a jumper, then Milan went ahead 30-28 on two free throws by Plump with 1:42 left. Craft missed a layup just under the one-minute mark that would have meant a four-point lead, and Muncie's Gene Flowers responded with a basket to tie the score. Plump held the ball until there were 18 seconds left and signaled for another timeout.

Wood set up the play: "Pass the ball into Plump," he said. "When Bobby crosses the line, everybody else clear to one side, away from him. Bobby, with about eight seconds to go, you start for the basket. Drive or shoot a jump shot, but don't shoot too early or they will have time to get another shot."

Plump almost gummed up the works by grabbing the ball out of bounds following the timeout. "I passed it to Craft and then he got the ball back to me," said Plump. "It wasn't exactly what Marvin wanted, but we never heard any complaints from him later."

As the other Milan players took up positions along the left sideline, Plump crossed mid-court and, with five seconds left, started his move against Jimmy Barnes, who, at 5-10, was about the same size as Plump. He faked left and drove right, creating enough daylight so he could pull up for a jumper from about 15 feet. It sailed through at the buzzer, giving tiny Milan the state championship.

"Yes, I knew," Plump said of his game-winning buzzer-beater. "When you shoot, you usually know when it's good."

Plump was named Indiana's "Mr. Basketball" for 1954 and went on to set scoring records at Butler and play AAU ball with the Phillips 66 Oilers, one of the best teams of that era. He participated in the 1960 U.S. Olympic Trials, but did not make the team.

"Our winning the state championship sure changed a lot of lives in Milan," said Plump, noting that nine of the 10 Milan players went on to attend college and eight graduated. "Not just for the 10 kids on the team, either. It opened up college to Milan kids for the next eight to 10 years."

"Any success I might have had in my lifetime after that had to do with us winning," said Craft, who played guard alongside Plump. "I got a scholarship to Butler. I became a teacher, a coach and an administrator (with the Indiana High School Athletic Association). I appreciate it."

00:40

· ·

Selvy's Memorable Miss

Frank Selvy always could score. While at Furman, he put up 100 points in a game against Newberry to set an NCAA Division I record that still stands, and when he left college in 1954, he held the career scoring record for Division I with 2,538 points. In his nine-year NBA career he scored more than 6,000 points and averaged 10.8 points per game, with a high of 19.0 ppg. In 1961-62, starting alongside Jerry West in the backcourt for the Los Angeles Lakers, he averaged 14.7 points, 5.2 rebounds and 4.8 assists per game.

But the shot Lakers fans will remember him for is the one he missed at the end of Game 7 of the 1962 NBA Finals. It's a shot Selvy can't forget, either.

"I would trade all my points for that last basket," said Selvy, whose eight-foot jumper from the left baseline rimmed out at the end of regulation, leaving the Lakers tied with the Boston Celtics at 100-100 in the deciding game of the series. Boston went on to win 110-107 in overtime, starting a frustrating eight-year period in which the Lakers would lose to the Celtics six times in the NBA Finals.

The Lakers were a team on the rise in 1961-62, their second season on the west coast after moving from Minneapolis. They had played well in the division finals the year before, stretching St. Louis to the seven-game limit, and built on that to compile a 54-26 record and win the Western Division title in 1961-62, finishing 11 games in front of Cincinnati. They beat the Detroit Pistons in six games to earn a berth in the NBA Finals, and were happy when Boston beat Philadelphia in seven games in the East because they had no center who could stop the dominant offense of Warriors center Wilt Chamberlain. They felt they matched up better against Boston and Bill Russell, who was brilliant on defense and as a rebounder but did not present the scoring threat Chamberlain did.

Elgin Baylor, limited to 48 games after being called up to Army reserve duty, averaged 38.3 points per game for the Lakers, second only to Chamberlain's 50.4 mark. What's more, his limited game time during the regular season left him fresh for the playoffs. "It was an enjoyable year," Baylor recalled. "Our camaraderie was great. On and off the court, we did things together. We enjoyed one another. As a team, we gave the effort every night."

Complementing Baylor's style of slashing to the basket was the brilliant jump shooting of West, who averaged 30.8 ppg in his second pro season. Rudy LaRusso, a 6-foot-8 Dartmouth product who was nicknamed "Roughhouse Rudy" by longtime (and highly partisan) Celtics announcer Johnny Most, started at the forward spot alongside Baylor, with Tom Hawkins coming off the bench. Selvy manned the guard position alongside West, with Hot Rod Hundley in reserve. Jim Krebs, 6-foot-8, and Ray Felix, 6-foot-11, were the team's centers.

It turned out to be a memorable NBA Finals. The Lakers won Game 2 129-122 for a split of the first two games at Boston Garden, and went home to a record crowd of 15,180 at the L.A. Sports Arena for a tense Game 3. West scored with four seconds to go, then stole Sam Jones' inbounds pass intended for Bob Cousy and laid it in at the buzzer for a 117-115 win that put the Lakers up 2-1.

Celtics coach Red Auerbach argued that it was impossible for West to dribble 30 feet and score so quickly, but the Laker star said he knew what he was doing when he ignored shouts from his own teammates to pull up for a jumper and continued in for the layup. "I had deflected the ball on the run," West explained. "I knew I would have enough time, because I knew what the shot clock was. Quite often I'm surprised today that more young players don't pay attention to the shot clock."

The Celtics bounced back to take Game 4 115-103 and regain the home-court advantage. In Boston for Game 5, Baylor put on an amazing one-man show, erupting for a finals-record 61 points and grabbing 22 rebounds as the Lakers again won on the road, 126-121. "Elgin was just a machine," marveled Satch Sanders, the Celtics' defensive ace who tried to shadow Baylor for most of the series.

The Lakers went home with a chance to end the series, but Boston would not allow it, winning Game 6 119-105 to send the series back to Boston for a winner-take-all seventh game.

The Celtics led 53-47 at halftime, but seven points by West in the final minute of the third quarter evened the score at 75-75 going into the fourth quarter. Boston moved in front 100-96, and when LaRusso was called for an offensive foul with one minute to go, the Celtics seemed in good shape. But Selvy grabbed a rebound and drove the length of the floor to score and cut the lead in half, then West stole a Cousy pass and fed it to Selvy, who this time missed his shot but grabbed his own rebound and scored to make it

100-100 with 18 seconds left. Ramsey drove toward the basket and tried a running hook shot over defenders but missed, and LaRusso grabbed the rebound and called a timeout with five seconds on the clock.

Coach Fred Schaus went to a three-guard lineup and put the ball in Hundley's hands, with Baylor the first option and West the second. But when play resumed, both of them were well covered. Hundley spotted Selvy open along the left baseline, since Cousy had left his man to double-team West. Hundley fired the pass to Selvy as Cousy scrambled to recover.

"It was a fairly tough shot," said Selvy. "I was almost on the baseline." His eight-footer bounced off the rim and the rebound was gobbled up by Russell, who totaled 30 points and 40 rebounds, sending the game into overtime. Baylor, for one, thought Boston had a little extra help on that final play of regulation.

"Selvy thought Bob Cousy fouled him, and I thought Cousy fouled him," said Baylor, who had 41 points in the game and finished the seven-game playoff series with 284 points, a record that still stands. "He took the shot from a spot where he was very proficient. But Cousy said he never fouled him. Then I was in a position to get the offensive rebound, but somebody behind me shoved me out of bounds right into the referee. There was no foul call there, either. I looked around and saw Russell and Sam Jones behind me." Baylor said he later watched the game film and saw that Jones had shoved him out of bounds, and when the two crossed paths, Jones admitted pushing him.

Nonetheless, with no foul call, the game went into overtime. The Celtics dominated the five-minute period, jumping in front early and holding on for a 110-107 victory as Sam Jones scored five of his 27 points in the extra session.

The Celtics had their fourth consecutive championship, and the Lakers had the bitter memory of Selvy's miss.

00:39

. . . .

Gonzaga Wears the Slipper with Attitude

Almost every year, some school comes from out of the pack and makes noise in the NCAA tournament, upsetting higher-seeded teams, wreaking havoc with office pools and capturing the imagination of casual followers as well as ardent fans.

In 1999 that school was Gonzaga, and this was one Cinderella team with attitude.

"There's a saying we have," said junior guard Richie Frahm. "If we get a glass slipper handed to us, we're going to crack it over your head."

The Bulldogs did just that in the NCAA West Regional. Gonzaga, a 10th-seeded afterthought, upset No. 7 Minnesota 75-63 and stunned No. 2 Stanford 82-74 to reach the Sweet Sixteen. Then they shocked No. 6 Florida 73-72 on Casey Calvary's tip-in with 4.4 seconds remaining to earn a berth in the Elite Eight, a first for the school in Eastern Washington that produced the NBA's career assists and steals leader, John Stockton—as well as a crooner of note named Bing Crosby.

That's when the coach turned back into a pumpkin, the coachmen into mice. Facing top-seeded and eventual national champion Connecticut, the Bulldogs fought gamely till the end but came up short, bowing 67-62.

"We didn't come in here scared of anybody," said Gonzaga guard Mike Nilson, reflecting the self-confidence that was a team trademark. "I expected to win every game."

"This team has great character and they are great kids," said coach Dan Monson. "There are a lot of teams at home with better basketball ability, but we get through that with chemistry and character."

"Do we belong?" said forward Mike Leasure, repeating a question about Gonzaga's first-ever trip to the Elite Eight. "Ask Florida if we belong."

That give-no-quarter attitude could be seen in the opening minutes of the game against Florida, when Calvary and the Gators' Major Parker exchanged elbows and pushes. After officials broke it up and Parker headed upcourt, Calvary followed him as if to continue the dispute.

"I have an anger management problem," Calvary conceded. "Sometimes I want to turn these games into a boxing match."

Florida, with a vaunted full-court press taught by Billy Donovan, who played and coached under Rick Pitino, was supposed to wear down the upstarts from Spokane, Washington, and the lightly regarded West Coast Conference. But in the end, when the game was on the line and time was running out, it was Gonzaga and Calvary who made the big play.

Seven three-pointers helped Gonzaga to a 35-34 halftime lead over the Gators, which it stretched to 52-44 with 14:08 left on a short jumper by Calvary, a 6-foot-8 sophomore. A 15-4 run put Florida in front, but Gonzaga was not about to be worn down. There were several ties and lead changes until Greg Stolt's three-pointer gave Florida a 72-69 advantage with 45.7 seconds left. Jeremy Eaton's lay-in with 19.7 seconds to play cut it to one, then Florida's Brent Wright, under intense defensive pressure, was called for a critical traveling violation with 15.4 seconds left before he could signal for a timeout.

"It hurts inside that I let the team down," said Wright. "I called the timeout but the ref said that I traveled. It's real sad. My heart just dropped with the traveling call."

Gonzaga called a timeout and Monson set up a play for either Frahm or Mike Santangelo to shoot. Instead, as might be expected for a team with attitude, Quentin Hall took a pass and drove into the lane for a lean-in jumper.

"I guess I just didn't listen," said Hall, whose shot bounced off the rim and backboard. That's when Calvary came to the rescue, charging into the lane, leaping over Wright and tipping the ball in.

"I had both hands on the ball," said Calvary. "The ball bounced around and it went in. I was nervous to get that shot off."

Then, attitude returning, he added, "I wanted to dunk it!"

To which Hall replied, "If Casey didn't get it and score, I was going to get it and score, so it really didn't matter. Do we belong? What kind of question is that? Yes, we belong!"

00:38

. . . .

Magic Fills in for the Big Fella

Time seemed to have run out on the Los Angeles Lakers.

Although they held a 3-2 lead over the Philadelphia 76ers in the 1980 NBA Finals, the Lakers' prospects had taken a definite turn for the worse when Kareem Abdul-Jabbar suffered a sprained ankle late in the third quarter of Game 5. The star center returned to action and scored 14 of his 40 points in the fourth quarter, including a tie-breaking three-point play with 33 seconds left that propelled the Lakers to a 108-103 victory, but when doctors took a look at his ankle after the game, they told him to forget about flying to Philadelphia the next morning for Game 6. Even recovery in time for a possible Game 7 was questionable, they said.

Abdul-Jabbar was the league's Most Valuable Player and the Lakers' mainstay, their leading scorer (24.8 ppg) and rebounder (10.8 rpg) and the top shot blocker (3.41 bpg) in the league. He had not missed a game all season, and Coach Paul Westhead was understandably worried about what effect Abdul-Jabbar's absence would have on his team—not just physically, but psychologically.

The Lakers had gone through the regular season with Jim Chones, their starting power forward, doubling as Abdul-Jabbar's backup at center. They didn't have another center on their roster; the best player on their bench was a guard, Michael Cooper. So rather than shift Chones into the middle (where he had played most of his career), Westhead turned to his rookie point guard, Earvin "Magic" Johnson, and told him he was needed to play center.

Johnson, of course, was not your typical point guard, nor your typical rookie.

He stood 6-9, taller than most forwards and just an inch or two below the height of the typical NBA center. And while, at age 20, his body was still in the process of filling out in terms of muscle, Johnson's brilliant ballhandling and special feel for the game already were very much in evidence. What's more, Johnson had played center in high school, which was only three years earlier, and though schoolboy center is a far cry from playing the pivot in the NBA, at least the nuances of the position weren't totally unfamiliar.

As for being a rookie, a boy amongst men, Johnson had turned that from a negative into a positive from the day he arrived in training camp. His ebullience on and off the court had invigorated the entire Laker organization and especially the 32-year-old Abdul-Jabbar.

In the very first game of his professional career, a last-second victory over the then-San Diego Clippers, Johnson had celebrated by leaping into the arms of a bewildered Abdul-Jabbar, much the way Yogi Berra did after Don Larsen pitched his perfect game in the 1956 World Series. Whoa, the Laker center had to tell the rookie, you'd better pace yourself. There are still 81 games to go, and that's just the regular season!

The Lakers, who went through a coaching change when Jack McKinney was injured in an early-season bicycle accident and replaced by Westhead, went on to win 60 games and the Pacific Division title in the regular season. They then beat Phoenix and defending-champion Seattle in five games apiece to advance to the NBA Finals against a strong Philadelphia team led by Julius Erving and also featuring Maurice Cheeks, Doug Collins and Darryl Dawkins. The first five games of the series were hard fought and close, with each being decided by 10 points or less, so the Lakers' 3-2 lead seemed offset by the injury to Abdul-Jabbar.

When the Lakers gathered at Los Angeles International Airport for the flight to Philadelphia for Game 6 and word spread that their team captain would not be joining them, Johnson decided to take matters into his own hands. He planted himself into Abdul-Jabbar's customary front-row aisle seat, stretched out and pulled a blanket over his head, just the way Abdul-Jabbar normally did. Then he winked at Westhead, turned to his teammates scattered about the first-class cabin and announced: "Never fear, E.J. is here!"

Johnson's attitude lifted his team's spirits, then he backed it up with one of the greatest performances in NBA Playoff history, getting 42 points, 15 rebounds, seven assists, three steals and a block as the Lakers beat the Sixers 123-107 to wrap up their first of five championships in the 1980s.

Johnson wore his trademark grin when he stepped into the center circle for the opening tip against Dawkins, and the Sixers were taken aback. The Lakers scored the first seven points of the game and went up 11-4 before Philadelphia seemed to wake up and realize the imposing presence of Abdul-Jabbar was missing from the Laker lineup. But with Steve Mix coming off the bench and slicing unimpeded toward the basket, Philadelphia rallied to take a 52-44 lead in the second quarter before going into halftime tied at 60-60.

Los Angeles scored the first 14 points of the third quarter, but again, Philadelphia fought back to close the gap, and with five minutes to play, the Lakers led by just 103-101. But Johnson scored nine points down the stretch, and Los Angeles outscored Philadelphia 20-6 to pull away and win.

In one of the best playoff performances nobody remembers, Lakers forward Jamaal Wilkes scored 37 points and grabbed 10 rebounds. But all the attention was focused on Johnson, the rookie who had seemed omnipresent, at one time or another playing every position on the court.

"What position did I play?" Magic said, repeating a reporter's question. "Well, I played center, a little forward, some guard. I tried to think up a name for it, but the best I could come up with was CFG-Rover."

"Magic was outstanding, unreal," said Doug Collins, who later would become an NBA head coach and TV commentator. "I knew he was good, but I never realized he was great."

After the game, Johnson looked into the TV cameras and sent a message to Abdul-Jabbar back in his home in Bel-Air: "We know you're hurtin', Big Fella, but we want you to get up and do a little dancin' tonight. This one's for you!"

00:37

Sampson Stops the Lakers

More than a decade before Tim Duncan and David Robinson led the San Antonio Spurs to the 1999 NBA Championship, another pair of Twin Towers ruled the Texas skyline. In the mid-1980s, 7-foot-4 Ralph Sampson and 7-foot Hakeem Olajuwon effectively teamed up for the Houston Rockets, leading them to the NBA Finals in 1986.

NBA coaches long have been intrigued with the idea of overwhelming opponents with a pair of giants. Early in 6-11 Nate Thurmond's career, he was used as a forward alongside 7-1 Wilt Chamberlain on the San Francisco Warriors. But when the team plummeted to the bottom of the Western Division in 1964-65, Chamberlain was traded to Philadelphia and Thurmond took over at center, where he blossomed into a Hall of Famer.

A similar scenario took place on the New York Knicks later in the '60s, when the club obtained 6-11 center Walt Bellamy and moved 6-10 Willis Reed over to forward. They played together for two full seasons, in which New York posted records of 36-45 and 43-39, but the Knicks didn't mesh into a championship unit until Bellamy was traded to Detroit for Dave DeBusschere in December 1968 and the center spot was given back to Reed.

Other teams have tried Twin Towers alignments, but until the Spurs matched Duncan up with Robinson, the one that was most successful was Houston's. And as with San Antonio, Houston enjoyed success with the Towers because both were unusual players.

Though he was one of the tallest players in NBA history, Sampson wasn't cut from the cloth of the traditional low-post pivotman. Lean and angular, he never had the weight or strength to muscle his way around the basket, but he was agile and could handle the ball and shoot from outside like a guard or forward. That unique combination of skills, plus his height and wingspan, enabled Sampson to earn the Rookie of the Year award in 1984 and Most Valuable Player honors at the 1985 NBA All-Star Game.

Much was expected of Sampson when he came into the NBA. "I don't think he'll be just great in the NBA, he'll be super-great," predicted the Boston Celtics' patriarch, Red Auerbach. NBA director of scouting Marty Blake said, "Ralph Sampson, coming out of college, is on par with any big man in the history of the game." And former coach and broadcaster Al McGuire added, "Six years from now, Ralph will be the best to have played this game." Sadly, long before that, knee injuries would take their toll; after three highly productive seasons with the Rockets, Sampson spent six frustrating seasons with Houston and three other NBA teams before retiring in 1992.

Olajuwon, who joined the Rockets one year after Sampson, has long been listed at 7 feet, although many believe he's closer to 6-10. But he has shown the strength to play center in the NBA for 15 seasons, and over the years has developed a remarkable array of spin-moves and drop-steps that have dazzled and frustrated opponents.

A perennial All-Star, Olajuwon led the Rockets to NBA titles in 1994 and 1995, when he was MVP of the finals both seasons. He also was the league's MVP in 1994, as well as its Defensive Player of the Year in 1993 and 1994, and is the NBA's career leader in blocked shots, although to be fair, it should be noted that blocks were not an official NBA statistical category in the days of Bill Russell.

Olajuwon and a healthy Sampson teamed for only two full seasons. In 1984-85, when Sampson was a second-year pro and Olajuwon a rookie, the Rockets compiled a 48-34 record and were eliminated by Utah in the first round of the playoffs. In 1985-86, Houston won the Midwest Division title at 51-31 and went all the way to the NBA Finals before bowing to the Boston Celtics in six games.

Along the way, the Rockets defeated the defending-champion Los Angeles Lakers in five games in the Western Conference Finals, Sampson nailing down the series with a last-second basket for a two-point win in Game 5. The 1986 finals marked the only time in a span of eight years, from 1982 through 1989, that the "Showtime" Lakers, led by Kareem Abdul-Jabbar and Magic Johnson, were0 stopped short of the NBA Finals.

Although the Rockets had beaten Sacramento and Denver in the first two rounds of the playoffs, they went into the Conference Finals as distinct underdogs to the Lakers, who were 62-20 in the regular season and had beaten the NBA's other two Texas teams, San Antonio and Dallas, in the playoffs. The Lakers had beaten Boston in the NBA Finals in 1985 after losing to them in 1984, and everyone was expecting a rubber match between the league's two most glamorous franchises. When the Lakers ripped Houston 119-107 in the series opener, there seemed no reason to think otherwise.

But Houston bounced back to steal a 112-102 victory at the Forum in Los Angeles, then went home and took firm command of the series with 117-109 and 105-95 decisions at the Summit. Suddenly, the Lakers found themselves on the brink of elimination, a very unfamiliar place for them to be.

Game 5 came down to a last shot in the closing seconds. With the score tied, the Rockets had the ball out of bounds in the frontcourt. Olajuwon, who had scored 30 points, had been ejected earlier in the game, leaving Sampson as the obvious primary option. Even the national TV cameras focused on Sampson when the Rockets broke their timeout huddle. As the referee handed the ball to Rodney McCray, Sampson worked his way into position against Abdul-Jabbar to the left of the lane. He caught the inbounds pass, turned and put up a high-arching fadeaway jumper that went in at the buzzer.

Houston had a 114-112 victory and the Lakers had been dethroned. Here's the call by CBS play-by-play announcer Dick Stockton:

"McCray will inbound, one second on the clock ... Sampson ... It goes! It's over! A miraculous shot by Ralph Sampson, off-balance, has given the Houston Rockets the Western Conference championship!"

That would prove to be the high-water mark for Sampson and the Twin Towers. The Rockets were beaten by Boston in six games in the 1986 NBA Finals, and injuries began to plague Sampson the following season, when he managed to start just 32 games. The Rockets moved him on to Golden State midway through the next season, and he never again achieved the level of success he had enjoyed as part of the Twin Towers in 1985 and 1986.

00:36

. . . .

The Birth of the NBA

Nobody knew quite what to expect when they arrived at Maple Leaf Gardens in Toronto on November 1, 1946. But the crowd of 7,090 that turned out to see the New York Knickerbockers play the Toronto Huskies in the debut of the Basketball Association of America, the forerunner of today's NBA, certainly was entertained as the teams fought through 48 minutes before the Knicks emerged with a 68-66 victory.

Basketball was a much different sport in those days. Most notably, it was played on the ground rather than in the air. The jump shot had yet to gain widespread acceptance. Forget about alley-oops or slam-dunks—set shots and layups were the order of the day. Also, there was no such thing as a shot clock, so players could take as long as they wanted to shoot. The result was a slower game that tended to get physical, since once a team had the lead, it often chose to freeze the ball and not attempt a shot, forcing the trailing team to foul in order to try to catch up.

Such matters did not concern the men who gathered at the old Hotel Commodore adjacent to New York's Grand Central Terminal on June 6, 1946. They knew that with World War II having recently ended, people were looking for peacetime diversions and willing to spend money to be entertained. While most of them were owners of hockey teams and/or the arenas in which they played and had little experience with basketball, they did know an opportunity when they saw one. Since college basketball was popular and its stars were graduating when fans were just getting to know them, why not start a professional basketball league to capitalize on this popularity? Such a league also would serve the purpose of filling dates when their arenas would otherwise sit empty, a not insignificant incentive.

Thus was born the Basketball Association of America, with 11 franchises: the Boston Celtics, New York Knickerbockers, Philadelphia Warriors, Providence Steamrollers, Toronto Huskies and Washington Capitols in the Eastern Division, and the Chicago Stags, Cleveland Rebels, Detroit Falcons, Pittsburgh Ironmen and St. Louis Bombers in the Western Division.

Ambitiously, the owners announced plans to begin play that fall. They basically adopted the rules of the college game—it wasn't until six weeks into the opening season that zone defenses were outlawed. One change they did make from the beginning was to lengthen the game by eight minutes, opting for four 12-minute quarters instead of two 20-minute halves in order to give the paying customers more entertainment for their money, at least in terms of minutes.

In keeping with the concept of capitalizing on the popularity of the college game, the teams relied heavily on players from schools in their geographic areas. The Knicks, for example, were composed largely of players from New York colleges, and their first coach, Neil Cohalan, came from Manhattan College. Teams practiced wherever they could; the Warriors, for example, went from one Philadelphia gym to the next, scrimmaging against the host team in exchange for workout time, while the Knicks used an out-of-season resort in the upstate Catskill Mountains.

The BAA schedule listed New York at Toronto as the only game on opening night. The day before the game, the Knicks took a train up to Canada, where they were met by a skeptical border guard. When Cohalan identified his troupe as the New York Knicks, the guard is said to have responded, "We're familiar with the New York Rangers. Are you anything like that?" When Cohalan came back with, "They play hockey, we play basketball," the guard replied, "I don't imagine you'll find many people up this way who'll understand your game—or have an interest in it."

That border guard turned out to be wrong, although it would take a while for the pro game to find a Canadian audience. The Huskies folded after one season, and while the Buffalo Braves played a number of their "home" games in Toronto in the 1970s, the city did not get another NBA franchise until 1995, when the Toronto Raptors began play.

Even back then the league was promotion-minded. The Huskies ran newspaper ads bearing a photo of 6-foot-8 George Nostrand, Toronto's tallest player, that asked, "Can You Top This?" The deal was that any fan taller than Nostrand would be granted free admission to the season opener; regular tickets were priced from 75 cents to $2.50, and there's no word on how many took advantage of the freebie.

"It was interesting playing before Canadians," said Sonny Hertzberg, one of the players for New York. "The fans really didn't understand the game at first. To them, a jump ball was like a face-off in hockey. But they started to catch on and seemed to like the action."

Not many details of that first game are known, because media coverage ranged from minimal to nonexistent. It is known that the first basket in league history was scored by New York's Ozzie Schectman on a layup. The Knicks recorded the first six points of the game and led 16-12 after one quarter and 37-29 at halftime. Early in the third quarter, Ed Sadowski, Toronto's 6-foot-5 player-coach, who already had scored a game-high 18 points, committed his fifth personal foul, and since the league was using college rules, he was forced to the bench for the rest of the game.

Nostrand replaced Sadowski and helped Toronto take its first lead of the game at 44-43, and the Huskies expanded the spread to 48-44 after three quarters. But the Knicks fought back and finally got a pair of baskets by Dick Murphy and a free throw by Tommy Byrnes in the final 2+ minutes to win 68-66. Leo Gottlieb was New York's leading scorer with 14 points.

The Washington Capitols, coached by a 29-year-old George Washington University graduate named Red Auerbach, who would later go on to great success with the Boston Celtics, compiled the best record in the league that inaugural season, going 49-11. But in an odd playoff system adopted from hockey, the two division champions faced each other in the first round of the playoffs, while the next four finishers competed in the other bracket, and Washington was eliminated by Western Division champion Chicago, four games to two. In the league's first championship series, the Stags were beaten by the Philadelphia Warriors four games to one. Joe Fulks of Philadelphia was the league's first scoring champion at 23.2 points per game.

The BAA, struggling for acceptance, admitted four teams from the midwest-based National Basketball League in 1948, including the best team in basketball, the Minneapolis Lakers, led by George Mikan and Jim Pollard. That signaled the end for the NBL, which had quality players but was composed of small-town franchises; its surviving teams joined the BAA for the 1949-50 season, when the league was renamed the National Basketball Association.

00:35

● ●

Imhoff Carries Cal to Title

The 1959 Final Four had everything a promoter could ask for, even though the two top-ranked teams in the nation, Kansas State and Kentucky, had been eliminated in the regionals.

In Oscar Robertson of Cincinnati and Jerry West of West Virginia, it had two of the greatest basketball players of all time. In the University of Louisville it had the hometown favorite, since the venue was Freedom Hall. And in California it had the underdog, a little-known team that stressed defense and fundamentals under the guidance of a man who was emerging as one of the game's great coaches, Pete Newell.

In later years, Newell would become famous for his Big Man's Camps, summer tutorials where centers and forwards from the professional and college ranks would gather to learn the fundamentals of footwork, the basics of boxing out. In the late '50s, Newell used his ability to shape and mold big men on Darrall Imhoff, who came to the Berkeley campus a gawky 6-foot-10 schoolboy and developed into a first-rate center who would anchor the United States' gold medal-winning 1960 Olympic team and go on to a 12-year pro career.

"Darrall Imhoff never lettered in high school," said Newell. "He broke his foot his freshman year at Cal, and I don't think he ever scored in double figures until he was a junior. So he was certainly not predicted to be much of a player his senior year, but he turned out to be a fine player."

Though Imhoff came to Newell with few credentials and little mobility, he had size and was willing to learn. Since he had an aptitude for shooting rather than muscling the ball into the basket, Newell worked on developing his soft touch on jump shots. And since he showed some quickness, Newell made that an integral part of his game, complementing his size. Those traits created problems for opponents, and ultimately denied fans the one-on-one dream matchup they were hoping for—Robertson vs. West, Cincinnati vs. West Virginia for the NCAA Championship.

Even as a senior, Imhoff didn't score a lot of points, but that wasn't necessary. The Golden Bears won by stopping teams from scoring, yielding a mere 51 points per game in 1959. But when California needed big baskets, Imhoff came through, scoring both the go-ahead basket in the national semifinals and the clinching bucket in the championship game.

The 6-foot-5 Robertson had led the nation in scoring at 32.6 points per game and could do it all—score from inside or out, pass, dribble, rebound. "There's never been one like him," said Hall of Fame coach Joe Lapchick. The 6-foot-2 West, like Robertson a junior, had averaged 26.6 ppg and also was a complete player, a shooter with great range who set up plays, rebounded and was his team's best defender. "If you sat down to build the perfect 6-foot-2 basketball player, you'd come up with Jerry West," said his coach, Fred Schaus. West had scored 69 points and grabbed 32 rebounds in games against St. Joseph's and Boston University in the East Regional, while Robertson's 24 points and 13 assists had led Cincinnati past top-ranked Kansas 85-75 in the Midwest Regional.

Neither would be enough to stop California, which had won its third successive Pacific Coast Conference title under the 43-year-old Newell, who stressed conditioning and even took his players out into the hills around campus for some roadwork during preseason. Such preparation enabled California to wear down opponents with a game-long full-court press that helped stymie higher-scoring foes.

Against Cincinnati in the semifinals, Newell's strategy was to keep Robertson from taking his man to the baseline and force him to spin toward the middle, where Imhoff and a weakside guard could help out. The strategy contained Robertson to 19 points and limited Cincinnati to 56 shots compared with California's 73, and while Cincinnati led 36-29 early in the second half, the Golden Bears managed to draw even at 54-54. That's when Imhoff blocked a shot attempt by Robertson and then scored a basket of his own to put California ahead to stay. The Golden Bears went on to win 64-58 and spoil the anticipated Robertson-West matchup in the final.

"We played excellent defense," said Newell. "We made Oscar work like the dickens for the ball. We made him bring the ball up and we did a really good job of defensive rotation. If we were going to get beat, we wanted those other guys to beat us."

That set up a meeting with West Virginia in the finals. How to stop West? Newell decided to try to prevent him from getting anything inside and force him to shoot from as far away from the basket as possible. West might still get his points, but he'd have to earn them with his marksmanship.

Despite being forced into a slower tempo than they would have liked, the Mountaineers still got off to a good start and led 23-13. But California's pressing defense and emphasis on giving West Virginia no easy baskets paid off as the Golden Bears rallied to take a 39-33 lead at halftime and extend that margin to 57-44 midway through the second half.

West, despite four personal fouls, went back into the game, and Schaus ordered West Virginia into a full-court press of its own. The normally poised Bears began to lose both their composure and the lead as the Mountaineers tried to play "beat the clock" in their comeback effort. But California had time on its side, and it also had Imhoff.

After West Virginia whittled the margin to 69-68 in the closing minute, Imhoff missed a shot attempt but used the moves and quickness Newell had taught him to collect his own rebound and put it back in for a 71-68 lead. With the three-point shot still nearly three decades away from finding its place in the college game, West Virginia was doomed. The Bears allowed Willie Akers to score an uncontested basket with seven seconds to play and then ran out the clock on a 71-70 victory.

West, who had 28 points and 11 rebounds against California and was voted Most Outstanding Player of the Final Four, was left with tears and an empty feeling as the championship trophy was presented to Al Buch, the Cal captain.

"I wasn't too proud to cry," he said. "What good are the fancy records and the high honors if you lose the championship by one point? I wouldn't want to play badly in any game or any tournament, but I'd rather have just played fair and had Imhoff or Oscar get the records and have my team get the title."

00:34

•••••••••••••••••••••••••••

Francis Tops, Selvy
Hits Century Mark

It's an achievement that time seems to have forgotten, yet it remains as impressive today as it was when it was done nearly half a century ago. On February 4, 1954, Clarence "Bevo" Francis of Rio Grande College set the all-time college basketball scoring record by pouring in 113 points against Hillsdale College.

Francis may be little known, but he was no flash in the pan. He actually scored more points, 116, in a game the previous season, but it didn't make the NCAA record book because it was not accomplished against a four-year college. And in 1953-54, Francis, in addition to his record-setting game against Hillsdale, also scored 84 points against Alliance and 82 against Bluffton. For the season, he averaged 46.5 points per game, another NCAA record.

Nine days after Francis posted his 113-point game, another collegian, Frank Selvy of Furman, poured in 100 points in a game against Newberry. Those two are the only 100-point performances in NCAA history.

The 6-foot-9 Francis came to Rio Grande along with his high school coach, Newt Oliver, in hopes that, through basketball, they could build up the tiny school in southeastern Ohio, whose enrollment dropped as low as 92 students one year. Oliver ambitiously announced he would take on all comers and Rio Grande went 39-0 in 1952-53, reportedly generating enough revenue to save the school from bankruptcy. The NCAA, however, dropped 27 of Rio Grande's wins from the record book, including one over Ashland (Kentucky) Junior College in which Francis scored 116 points, because they came against military teams, junior colleges and vocational schools rather than four-year colleges.

Oliver and Francis were upset by what they viewed as a slight on the part of the NCAA as they began the 1953-54 season. "I never cared much about points before, but I really did want to break 100 sometime this year," Francis said after he achieved his goal.

Late in the season, Oliver looked at Rio Grande's schedule and saw a game in which Francis might be able to go for the century mark. The team was to play Hillsdale, which had earlier been trounced by Rio Grande 82-45. "With only seven games to go, I became more determined than ever that Bevo would again go over the 100-point mark," said Oliver. "This was the game that was to be heard 'round the world."

Francis had 43 points at halftime, which was good, but not good enough for the century mark, unless he picked up the pace. So Oliver ordered his players not to worry about the team score but to focus on setting up Francis every time Rio Grande got the ball in the second half. He also told his players to foul any Hillsdale player who tried to kill time off the clock and thus prevent Francis from reaching 100.

Rio Grande's players followed Oliver's instructions to the letter. In those days college games were played in four 10-minute quarters instead of two 20-minute halves, and Francis scored 31 of his team's 33 points in the third period to raise his total to 74. Then, in the fourth quarter, he scored 39 of his team's 43 points to finish the game with 113, as Hillsdale coasted to a 134-91 victory.

"I really don't remember much about the 113-point game," said Francis. "It was just another time when I was double-and triple-teamed. Their coach told me after that game that if he could have dressed, he would have guarded me, too.

"I didn't know I had gotten 113 points until I was coming out of the shower after the game and a couple of players told me. I knew I'd been shooting well, but getting 113 points! I had no idea. I still can't believe it."

Francis left Rio Grande after his sophomore year, record in hand, and joined the team that played against the Harlem Globetrotters on their barnstorming trips. He was drafted by Philadelphia of the NBA in 1956, but couldn't reach agreement on a contract and thus never went on to play NBA ball.

The modern NCAA record book lists Francis's feat as the scoring standard for Division II. The Division III mark of 69 points was set by Steve Diekmann of Grinnell against Simpson in 1995, while there are two records listed for Division I, the major colleges. Kevin Bradshaw of U.S. International owns the mark for most points against a Division I opponent, 72 points against Loyola Marymount on January 5, 1971. And Selvy holds the record for most points against a non-Division I opponent, 100 against Newberry on February 13, 1954.

Selvy, whose scoring average of 41.7 points per game for the 1953-54 season ranks fourth in NCAA Division I annals behind Pete Maravich's three varsity years, was an outstanding jump shooter who went on to a nine-year career as an NBA guard, twice making the All-Star team and averaging 10.8 points per game for his pro career.

The game against Newberry was televised throughout the state of South Carolina, a first for Furman basketball. Selvy's mother, who had never seen her son play in college, came to Greenville, South Carolina for the game. It figured to be a big night.

Selvy scored 24 points in the first quarter, Newberry defender Bobby Bailey fouling out after just 2:43 had gone by. Selvy added 13 points in the second quarter for 37 at the half, at which point

Furman coach Lyles Alley followed Oliver's lead by ordering his players to set up Selvy on every second-half possession.

Selvy tallied 26 of his team's 32 points in the third quarter, giving him 63 going into the final 10 minutes. Then he poured in 37 of his team's 40 in the fourth quarter to finish with an even 100 as Furman romped, 149-95.

He reached the century mark at the last possible second, on a buzzer-beating heave from the opposite key some 70 feet away.

"It was my night, because that ball went right through the basket and hit nothing but net," said Selvy. "It was one of those shots where more luck than skill was involved. But when a player scores 100 points, there has to be plenty of both. It was something that was just meant to be."

00:33

• •

Notre Dame Stops UCLA's Winning Streak at 88

UCLA's feat of winning 10 NCAA championships in 12 years may be even more remarkable than the Boston Celtics' winning 11 NBA titles in 13 years. While Bill Russell was the mainstay of the Celtics' dynasty, playing on all 11 championship teams, and several other players were on half a dozen or more of those clubs, the roster of the Bruins was constantly changing, since players only were eligible for three varsity seasons.

For UCLA, the constant factor was the man on the end of the bench, the head coach known as the Wizard of Westwood, John Wooden. A standout high school and college player in Indiana, Wooden coached for 29 seasons, the last 27 of them at UCLA, compiling a career record of 664-162, including 620-147 at UCLA, before retiring after winning his 10th NCAA championship in 1975.

After UCLA beat Kentucky 92-85 in the 1975 NCAA title game, sending Wooden into retirement a winner, Bruins forward Dave Meyers declared, "I played my heart out for coach Wooden. It meant that much to me. He deserves to go out a winner."

To which Wooden dryly replied, "I suppose anyone would like to go out with a victory. The fact that the victory was for the national championship doesn't lessen the pleasure."

Victories were the standard bill of fare at UCLA's Pauley Pavilion starting in 1963-64, when Wooden led the Bruins to a perfect 30-0 mark and their first NCAA crown. That began a 12-year span in which UCLA lost a total of just 22 games, and eight of them came in 1965-66, when Kareem Abdul-Jabbar (then known as Lew Alcindor) was a freshman and ineligible to compete for the Bruin varsity. Eliminate that season and you have 14 losses in 11 years–barely more than one per season!

UCLA had four 30-0 seasons in that stretch and won 10 NCAA championships, including seven in a row from 1966-67 through 1972-73. And from January 30, 1971, through January 17, 1974, the Bruins set an NCAA record by winning 88 consecutive games.

That streak might have been considerably longer, but Notre Dame, behind 46 points by Austin Carr, had defeated UCLA 89-82 on January 26, 1971, ending a 47-game Bruin winning streak. That left UCLA short of the record of 60 consecutive wins set by the University of San Francisco team that featured Russell and K.C. Jones.

UCLA immediately began another winning streak, and this

time it would get the record—and Notre Dame would be its victim in consecutive win No. 61. On January 28, 1973, with the record on the line, the Bruins were determined not to let it get away as they jumped out to a 61-39 lead midway through the second half and coasted to an 82-63 victory. Center Bill Walton had a triple-double in the record-setting victory, getting 16 points, 15 rebounds and 10 blocked shots.

Nearly one year later, the winning streak was up to 88 games when UCLA faced Notre Dame once again on January 19, 1974. The Bruins were ranked No. 1, as usual, but the Irish were ranked No. 2 with a team that featured future pros Adrian Dantley, John Shumate and Gary Brokaw. Making UCLA's situation all the more precarious was the fact that Walton had suffered a back injury earlier in the month and had not played in 12 days.

Once the game started, however, Walton looked as unstoppable as ever. He connected on 12 of his first 13 shots and dominated the middle, helping UCLA to a seemingly comfortable 70-59 lead with just 3+ minutes remaining in the game.

At that point, Wooden ordered his team out of its usual offense and into a delay game. This attempt to kill the clock backfired, however; all it killed was UCLA's momentum.

Notre Dame countered by going into a full-court press, and the defense rattled the Bruins, who suddenly began turning the ball over. Shumate scored a pair of baskets and Dantley and Brokaw added one apiece, and suddenly UCLA's 11-point lead was down to three. After another Bruin turnover, Brokaw scored again to make it 70-69 with 1:11 left on the clock. Notre Dame had sliced 10 points off the lead in less than two minutes.

UCLA forward Jamaal Wilkes was called for a charging foul, giving the ball back to Notre Dame. It was the fifth consecutive possession on which the Bruins had turned the ball over, and it was all the opportunity the Irish would need. But while everyone was expecting one of Notre Dame's three stars to attempt the shot to take the lead, it was a member of the supporting cast who stepped into the spotlight and became the hero.

"We wanted Shumate and Brokaw to set up a two-on-one situation on one side, because they had been so effective," said Dwight Clay, the other guard alongside Brokaw in the Notre Dame lineup. "Curtis Rowe began to cheat and help Wilkes stop their action. That left me alone in the corner and I waved my hands. Brokaw read it and got me the ball."

In the right corner, Clay caught the pass and went right up with his jumper that sailed through with 29 seconds left on the clock. "I knew it was good as soon as it left my hands," said Clay, whose basket gave Notre Dame a 71-70 victory and ended the longest winning streak in college basketball history.

00:32

· ·

How a Tennis Racket Helped DeMatha Beat Power Memorial

Kareem Abdul-Jabbar, then known as Lew Alcindor, was 6-feet-8 when he graduated elementary school and grew to over 7 feet while at Power Memorial, a Catholic high school on Manhattan's West Side. As a freshman, he was rail-thin and gangly, and his first scrimmage against Erasmus, one of the city's top public school teams, was "a disaster," according to Abdul-Jabbar, who took it hard. "We were destroyed and I looked awful. After the game I sat in the locker room and cried, like a gigantic baby sitting there weeping. I hated to lose, and I absolutely hated to look bad doing it."

Burning with pride and a desire to succeed, Abdul-Jabbar made sure it would not often be repeated. During his freshman year, he grew and matured, both physically and emotionally, learning how to use both his height and his athletic skills to best advantage. His team lost six games during his freshman year, but by the time he began his sophomore season, he was being touted as not just an All-City candidate but a possible All-American.

Abdul-Jabbar lived up to the billing, and then some. He dominated high school and college basketball for the next seven years, then went on to a 20-year professional career in which he led his teams to six championships and became the all-time leading scorer in National Basketball Association history.

For all his success and acclaim as a professional, it was on the scholastic level that he was most dominant. His freshman team at UCLA (first-year students were not eligible for varsity teams in those days) went 21-0 as Abdul-Jabbar averaged 33.1 points and 21.5 rebounds per game. The frosh even beat the varsity, a team that was ranked No. 1 and was the defending national champion, by 15 points in a preseason scrimmage. Then, in his three varsity seasons, Abdul-Jabbar led UCLA to a stunning 86-2 record and three national championships, earning All-America honors every year as he averaged 26.4 points and 15.5 rebounds per game for his college career.

He was equally successful, if not more so, at Power Memorial High School. His team won 71 consecutive games in one stretch, a streak that was broken in his senior year by DeMatha Catholic High School, a perennial power from the Washington suburb of Hyattsville, Maryland, that dealt Power and Abdul-Jabbar the only loss of his last three years in high school. "They were a good, well-trained team with a winning tradition and the serious desire to beat our behinds," Abdul-Jabbar said of DeMatha.

The man behind the training and the winning tradition was Morgan Wooten, who has amassed well over 1,000 victories since becoming basketball coach at DeMatha in 1956. While his teams have won over 85 percent of their games, been chosen national champions on several occasions and produced many future college and pro stars, the single game Wooten and DeMatha are best known for is that win over Power Memorial in 1965.

"It was the high school game of the year in the nation, maybe of all time," said Wooten, whose team took a 29-game winning streak into the showdown against Power and its 71-game skein. "They beat us the year before in the last minute by three points, and Kareem scored 38 points. Our strategy in the 1964 game was to let Kareem score whatever he could while we stopped everybody else. For the '65 rematch, I reversed our strategy: We would try to stop Kareem. The other Power players would have to pick up the slack, if they could. If they couldn't, we would win."

Ah, but how to stop Abdul-Jabbar, as dominant a player as high school basketball has ever seen, one who towered over his opponents both literally and figuratively?

Offensively, Wooten figured that by having two or three players collapse on Abdul-Jabbar every time he caught the ball, DeMatha could keep his point total down. But he was worried about the effect the 7-2 youngster would have at the other end of the floor. Could his players adjust to the imposing defensive presence of Abdul-Jabbar, whose height made him a threat to block so many shots?

Wooten was looking for some way to teach his players what it would be like to go against such a tall opponent and thought about having his best player, 6-foot-8 Sid Catlett, stand on a chair in the lane. John Moylan, a friend of Wooten's who later became the principal at DeMatha, suggested using a tennis racket instead.

By putting the racket in Catlett's hands and letting him get off the chair and roam the court, it allowed Wooten to simulate not just Abdul-Jabbar's size but his mobility. "Sid had firm orders from me to block every shot he could," said Wooten. "With his height and that tennis racket added to it, he looked like the Washington Monument in a DeMatha uniform. With his jumping ability added to everything else, our shooters had to put enough arch on their shots to bring rain."

"DeMatha came prepared," recalled Abdul-Jabbar. "They had two 6-foot-8 big men, Bob Whitmore and Sid Catlett, who both went on to play at Notre Dame, and they sandwiched me, tried to deny me the ball. They slowed the game down, walked the ball up the court when they had it, and double- and triple-teamed me on our end. The game was close, but they played well, made the crucial shot at the end, and won it 46-43."

"We did it by stopping Abdul-Jabbar and taking away Power's inside game, holding him to 16 points, 14 below his average," said Wooten. "And by being able to score over him, thanks to John Moylan and his tennis racket."

00:31

•••••••••••••••••••••••••

Showdown in the Astrodome: Houston Beats UCLA

If one game can be said to have taken college basketball out of the band-box campus gyms and into the big fancy arenas, making it a major part of the American sports scene, it was the showdown between UCLA and Houston in the Astrodome on January 20, 1968.

It was a game that had everything: No. 1 UCLA vs. No. 2 Houston, defending national champions vs. hometown heroes in a clash of unbeatens. It also featured two consensus All-Americans, Kareem Abdul-Jabbar (then known as Lew Alcindor) and Elvin Hayes, in a matchup of future Hall of Famers.

Most of all, it was a spectacle.

The game attracted a crowd of 52,693, the largest ever to see a basketball game to that point. None of them were seated within 100 feet of the court, which had been trucked to Houston from Los Angeles and set up where second base normally would have been— at the center of the nearly circular building. Only the Astrodome's permanent seats were used, other than tables and chairs for scorers, officials and media, meaning the players looked minuscule from even the best seat in the house—yet no one seemed to mind.

The buildup for this game had been tremendous. UCLA had won 47 consecutive games, including a 79-64 win over Dayton in the 1967 NCAA championship game, and had never been beaten with the 7-foot-2 Abdul-Jabbar, a junior, in the lineup. Houston also was undefeated, having won 17 straight games since bowing to the Bruins 73-58 in the Final Four the previous spring, and was led by the 6-foot-9 Hayes, a senior.

Abdul-Jabbar had suffered a scratched left cornea eight days earlier in a game against California. "The pain was overwhelming, but worse than that, I couldn't see. I had double vision, and those images that did get through were blurred and teary," he said. Abdul-Jabbar spent three days in a darkened hospital room, missing two games, and wore an eye patch for most of the week leading up to the showdown. He was unable to practice with the team and lost the fine edge in timing, coordination and conditioning that sepa-rates great athletes from the rest.

"I knew my depth perception was totally shot, but I thought I could make up for it by rebounding and playing good defense," said Abdul-Jabbar. "Unfortunately, I overestimated myself, and so did Coach (John) Wooden. The game wasn't five minutes old before I was exhausted, and I had no second wind."

Hayes, meanwhile, was on fire, scoring 29 points in the first half alone. Houston led by as many as 15 points in the first half, but by just 46-43 at intermission. The pace of the second half was more deliberate, and with 3:02 to play, the score was tied 65-65. Hayes scored on a baseline jumper and teammate Don Chaney added a 15-footer to make it 69-65, but UCLA guard Lucius Allen hit a basket and two free throws to tie the score at 69-69 with 44 seconds left.

"The fans knew they were seeing a game for the history books, one every bit as good as the buildup," said Hayes. "The players were aware of it, too. We knew we were taking part in one of the greatest games ever played, and not just because of all the ingredients going into it. The greatest game was being played as the perfect game."

With the score tied, Houston worked the ball to Hayes down low, to the left of the basket. He moved toward the corner for a turnaround jumper and was fouled by Jim Nielsen with 28 seconds left. Though he was just a 60 percent free-throw shooter, Hayes stepped to the line and sank both shots for a 71-69 lead. Houston went into a full-court press, and UCLA's inbounds pass went out of bounds off one of the Bruins. Houston got the ball inbounds, and Hayes ran some time off the clock before passing to George Reynolds, who held onto the ball until the buzzer sounded. Hayes and Reynolds both leaped in the air and embraced, then the fans came pouring onto the floor of the Astrodome and onto the court, where they lifted Hayes onto their shoulders.

Hayes finished with 39 points on 17-for-25 from the field. He added 15 rebounds and 8 blocked shots. Abdul-Jabbar, meanwhile, had 15 points and 12 rebounds but shot a woeful 4-for-18 from the field. Afterward, when writers mentioned to Hayes that it was clear that Abdul-Jabbar was hampered by the eye injury, he would have none of it.

"I don't want to hear another word about how Lew Alcindor's eye injury affected his play and cost UCLA the victory," declared Hayes. "Last year, when they beat us in the tournament, I didn't make any excuses. It was one of those nights when a particular team just seemed to be picked by destiny to win. That night it happened to be Houston."

Both teams knew, however, that there might well be another night. The NCAA Final Four would be played in Los Angeles in a little more than two months, and a semifinal matchup between UCLA, from the West Regional, and Houston, from the Midwest, seemed a distinct possibility. "I hope they come back to L.A. undefeated," said Allen, voicing the feeling of the entire UCLA squad. "That would be very nice."

As it happened, both teams did not lose again until they met in the NCAA Semifinals. This time Houston was No. 1, UCLA No. 2. The Bruins had thought about little but this rematch as they watched Houston get the headlines and Hayes earn Player of the Year honors. They were out for revenge, and they got it.

UCLA used a diamond-and-one defense, with Lynn Shackelford shadowing Hayes wherever he went and Abdul-Jabbar stationed under the basket. Hayes managed just 10 points, and without a big game from him the Cougars had little chance against the deeper Bruins. UCLA was unstoppable on offense, racing to an early 41-24 lead and coasting to a 101-69 victory. "We beat them by 32 points and settled that argument," said Abdul-Jabbar. All five Bruin starters tallied in double figures: Abdul-Jabbar, Allen and Mike Lynn scored 19 apiece, Shackelford had 17 and Mike Warren had 14.

"The championship game was like an afterthought," said Abdul-Jabbar, who scored 34 points and hauled down 16 rebounds as UCLA beat North Carolina 78-55 for the second of what would turn out to be seven consecutive NCAA championships.

Wooden, when asked to compare his many great UCLA clubs, said, "It would be hard to pick a team over that 1968 team. I will say it would be the most difficult team to prepare for and play against offensively and defensively. It created so many problems. It had such great balance."

But for one night, it came out second best in the game that put college basketball front and center on the sports map.

00:30

· ·

Cheryl Miller Leads Southern Cal to Title— with Flair

Some fantastic finishes come without a single point being scored. Case in point: Southern Cal's victory over Louisiana Tech in the 1983 NCAA women's championship game at the Scope in Norfolk, Virginia.

The Lady Trojans, led by future Hall of Famer Cheryl Miller, then a 6-foot-2 freshman, had a 69-67 lead and the ball when Rhonda Windham was called for a charging foul, her fifth of the game. That gave possession to Louisiana Tech, the defending NCAA champion, with 1:26 to play. But Miller came up big defensively, blocking a shot by Tia Sossamon, and Southern Cal recovered.

Cynthia Cooper tried to stretch Southern Cal's lead to four points but missed her layup attempt and Louisiana Tech had another chance to tie. Debra Rodman missed a shot and grabbed her own offensive rebound, but before she could attempt a put-back, Cooper stripped the ball from behind and Southern Cal got it back with 39 seconds on the clock.

Kathy Doyle of USC then tried to dribble away as much of the remaining time as possible, but this time it was Tech that made the big defensive play as Kim Mulkey reached in from behind and tipped the ball to Rodman. As soon as she knocked the ball away, Mulkey turned and raced upcourt, and Rodman tossed her a perfect lob pass. But Cooper made another outstanding defensive play, beating Mulkey down the floor and drawing a charging foul with nine seconds left to play that was hotly contested by the Lady Techsters.

"That was a bad call," said Louisiana Tech coach Leon Barmore. "I'm not going to criticize the officials, but the call was not a good one."

Forced to foul, Tech put the freshman Miller on the line with six seconds on the clock. But Miller, who had a brilliant game with 27 points, nine rebounds, four steals and four blocks and had scored the go-ahead basket on a jumper with 7:10 to play, missed the front end of a one-and-one, giving Louisiana Tech one last chance. Rodman rebounded and fed a pass to Mulkey, but before she could get into position to shoot or pass to another teammate, the buzzer sounded. Southern Cal had survived four late scoring chances and dethroned Louisiana Tech 69-67.

Southern Cal used a full-court press in the second half to erase a 37-26 deficit at intermission. "We were playing Tech's game," said Miller, who, along with Cooper, played a key role as the Trojans picked up the pace in the second half and got back into their productive running attack.

"I told them if they created the press and played hard, they'd get back in their tempo," said Southern Cal coach Linda Sharp. "I think we really surprised them with the press. I don't think they were talking about the press at halftime."

Southern Cal's scrambling defense checked Louisiana Tech center Janice Lawrence, who had 17 points in the first half but just three following the break. "We certainly can't win if Janice Lawrence doesn't get the basketball," said Barmore. "Their press is part of the reason she did not get it as much as we would have liked. We did not handle it very well at critical times."

"We couldn't have come back to win any other way," said Cooper. "I really liked the trust she showed in me by letting me upbeat the tempo."

Miller was named the tournament's outstanding player, capping a great freshman year for the highly recruited woman who had averaged 32.8 points and 15.0 rebounds in four years at Riverside Poly High School in Riverside, California, and who once scored 105 points in a game against Norte Vista High School, the most ever by a female high school player.

A fiery competitor, Miller led Southern Cal to another title in 1984, when she again was the outstanding player of the tournament. She also helped the United States to its first gold medal at the 1984 Olympics in Los Angeles, and later led the U.S. to victory in the World Championships and the Goodwill Games.

The older sister of NBA star Reggie Miller, Cheryl was an All-American all four years at Southern Cal and a three-time National Player of the Year who played a major role in the growth of women's basketball because of both her success and the way she played the game—with flair and flamboyance, boldness and brashness that came from growing up playing against boys on the playgrounds of Southern California.

"Cheryl has revolutionized the game," said Nancy Lieberman-Cline, another Hall of Famer and a pioneer of the women's game who led Old Dominion to college championships in 1979 and 1980. "She's taught young girls to play hard all the time and to be physical. She learned to do that the same way I did—we had to play like the guys.

"The flamboyance is her bread and butter. She sees those cameras and she seizes the moment. I think Cheryl is the best thing that could have happened to the game."

Miller later coached at Southern Cal and became a popular broadcaster for ABC and Turner Sports. She was inducted into the Hall of Fame in 1995, and in November 1996 she became the first female analyst to work a nationally televised NBA game. When the WNBA was founded, she became the first head coach and general manager of the Phoenix Mercury.

00:29

• •

It's Miller Time!

When seconds count, it's Miller Time. That's Reggie Miller, shooting guard of the Indiana Pacers.

"I've always considered myself a crunch-time player," said Miller. "The more eyes that are on you, the more intense you become."

Many players play better at home, where they are in comfortable surroundings and the fans are supporting them, than on the road, where the settings are different and the fans are against them.

Many players play better during the regular season—when the toughest thing to overcome is the 82-game grind of travel, practice, play, then do it all over again—than in the playoffs, when opponents, fans and media turn up the spotlight and every move is scrutinized, every mistake magnified.

Many players play better during the first 47 minutes and change of an NBA game, when errors can be redeemed, than in the closing seconds, when the next opportunity likely will be your last.

Reggie Miller is the opposite. He thrives on the road, in the playoffs, when the game is on the line, to the point where he entitled his autobiography *I Love Being the Enemy.*

"There's got to be people that everyone loves to hate. I just happen to be that person," said Miller, who feeds off opposing fans' frenzy. "Every time they start to chant my name, it gets me going more and more.

"I respect and I like when fans get into the game. That's part of professional sports. I like wearing the black hat. I'm not always going to have great games on the road, but why not try?"

Why not, indeed. The essence of competition is rising to meet a challenge, and the greater the challenge, the greater the competitor who meets it. Michael Jordan, for all his talents, was supremely competitive, a man who hated to lose, whether it was at basketball or blackjack, golf or go fish. Larry Bird and Jerry West also come to mind. Miller, too, is just such a competitor.

But just being competitive is not enough. To make a great enemy, you have to be able to back up your bravado, to walk the walk. And Miller repeatedly has done that, especially against the New York Knicks, for whom he has become the arch enemy.

- In one of the most amazing playoff finishes of all time, he scored eight points in the last 16.4 seconds, rallying the Pacers from a 105-99 deficit to a 107-105 victory over the Knicks in Game 1 of the 1995 Eastern Conference Semifinals at Madison Square Garden.

- He scored 25 points in the fourth quarter, hitting five three-point field goals, and scored 39 points overall in Game 5 of the 1994 Eastern Conference Finals as the Pacers beat the Knicks 94-86, again at the Garden. After one of his threes, he turned to Knicks courtside regular Spike Lee and wrapped his hands around his neck in a mock choking sign.
- After missing eight games due to an eye injury, Miller returned to the lineup and scored 29 points in a deciding Game 5 play-off loss to Atlanta in 1996, getting 16 of his points in the fourth quarter.
- He scored 38 points, including a three-pointer with 5.9 seconds left to force overtime that he hit from directly in front of Spike Lee's courtside seat at the Garden. The Pacers went on to beat the Knicks 118-107 in Game 4 of the 1998 Eastern Conference Semifinals.
- Despite a badly sprained ankle, Miller sank a three-pointer with 0:00.7 on the clock as the Pacers beat the Chicago Bulls 96-94 in Game 4 of the Eastern Conference Finals.

Here's a remarkable stat that shows Miller's ability to come through in the clutch: In the 1998 regular season and playoffs, he attempted 14 game-winning or game-breaking shots; he made 12 of them.

"You can't be scared to fail," he said. "You're not going to make every shot or every play, but you can believe that you can. I think that's my strongest attribute—I believe that I can."

And doing it on the stage of the NBA Playoffs, especially if it happens to be in a place like Madison Square Garden, makes it that much more enticing. "Whatever you do during the regular season is nice," said Miller, "but kids talk about you on the playgrounds because of what you do during the playoffs."

Jordan averaged 1.9 more points per game during the playoffs than the regular season. West, the original "Mr. Clutch" and a boyhood idol of Miller's growing up in Riverside, California, was plus 2.1. Elvin Hayes was plus 1.9, Walt "Clyde" Frazier plus 1.8, Rick Barry plus 1.6, John Havlicek, Sam Jones and Isiah Thomas plus 1.2 apiece.

Many players wind up on the minus side of that comparison, because in a best-of-7 playoff series, opponents can focus their defenses against a star and can practice shutting him down day after day. Wilt Chamberlain averaged 7.6 points per game less in the playoffs that in the regular season and Oscar Robertson was minus 3.5, yet clearly both are among the game's all-time elite.

Miller is plus 3.3.

"When I look at players (for trades or the draft), one of the things I do is look at how they do in the playoffs as opposed to the regular season," said Pacers president Donnie Walsh. "A lot of players go down in the playoffs, but Reggie's the reverse. That shows the greatness in players, when they can go up to that level. That's when the money's on the line, so to speak.

"When the game is on the line, he's got to be in the top five guys you want shooting the ball."

Miller had an edge growing up. Not only did he play against the boys in his neighborhood, he also played against older sister Cheryl, a future Hall of Famer. That honed his competitiveness, as well as his skills, as he used to fantasize about taking the game-winning shot.

"Every kid has done it," said Miller. "You're counting 5, 4, 3, 2, 1, and imagining so-and-so is guarding you. When I walk onto the court with 10 seconds left, I'm thinking about that."

Miller attended UCLA, whose Pauley Pavilion was often used by Lakers such as Magic Johnson for pickup games. Miller used to love to soak it all in.

"They would talk about how when the playoffs came around, it was a different intensity," he recalled. "They talked about how it was a different season, a different mentality. You become edgier, meaner. Every possession counts. From that point on, I tried to envision how the playoffs would be for myself. It's always clicked when the playoffs came around, how you had to become a different person and a different player."

For Miller, it's meant becoming the enemy, wearing the black hat—a role he plays to perfection—and making every second count.

00:28

• •

The New York Knicks' Miracle Finishes

Befitting one of the NBA's three remaining original franchises (along with the Boston Celtics and the Philadelphia/Golden State Warriors), the New York Knicks have had their share of buzzer-beaters and great comebacks over the years.

In their first championship season, the Knicks scored six points in the final 16 seconds of play—basket, steal, basket, steal, basket —to wipe out a five-point deficit and beat the then-Cincinnati Royals 106-105 on November 28, 1969, the final game in what was then an NBA-record 18-game winning streak.

In their only other championship season, New York put the clamps on the Milwaukee Bucks and Kareem Abdul-Jabbar, not allowing a point in the final 5:11 of the game while running off 19 points of their own for an 87-86 victory on November 18, 1972.

On Martin Luther King Day, January 15, 1990, with one-tenth of a second on the clock, Trent Tucker caught an inbounds pass in front of the scorer's table and nailed a three-pointer to beat the Chicago Bulls 109-106. That controversial basket would not have counted today; the Bulls' protests led the NBA to adopt the "Trent Tucker rule" which dictates that there must be at least three-tenths of a second on the clock in order for anything but a tip-in to be legal.

The Knicks have also had their share of dramatic moments at other times, such as the game in 1962, when Wilt Chamberlain burned them for 100 points in Hershey, Pennsylvania, or Game 7 of the 1970 NBA Finals, when injured center Willis Reed hobbled onto the floor during pre-game warm-ups, scored New York's first two baskets of the game and provided the inspirational lift needed to carry them past the Los Angeles Lakers 113-99 for their first NBA championship.

For sustained drama, however, the Knicks may have topped themselves with their improbable run from obscurity to the NBA Finals in 1999.

The Knicks were languishing at 21-21 after losing to the Philadelphia 76ers 72-67 on April 19, leaving them battling Charlotte and Cleveland just to make the playoffs. The next day, team president and general manager Ernie Grunfeld was relieved of his duties. With two weeks left in the season, the Knicks were a team in turmoil. But with Latrell Sprewell and Marcus Camby, both of whom had been acquired in off-season trades engineered by Grunfeld, playing increasingly important roles and veteran Patrick Ewing coming through with some big games, the Knicks won six of their final eight games to capture the last Eastern Conference playoff berth by one game over the Hornets.

That set up the Knicks against the top-seeded Miami Heat in the first round of the playoffs, two teams with a history between them. Miami coach Pat Riley used to coach the Knicks, but left amidst acrimony for greener pastures. Knicks coach Jeff Van Gundy used to be Riley's assistant in New York; his brother, Stan Van Gundy, was now Riley's assistant in Miami. In 1997, New York blew a 3-1 series lead and bowed to Miami in a seven-game Eastern Conference semifinal series marred by a bench-clearing brawl in the pivotal Game 5. In 1998 it was Miami that blew a 2-1 series lead and bowed to New York in a five-game first-round series, the Knicks whipping the Heat 98-81 in Miami in the deciding game after Heat star Alonzo Mourning had been suspended for fighting.

Only once in NBA history had an eighth-seeded team knocked off a No. 1 seed, Denver doing it to Seattle in 1994. But 1998-99 was an unusual season, the schedule shortened to 50 games in 90 days due to the labor dispute and lockout that delayed the start of the season by some three months. Only six games separated No. 1 Miami, 33-17, from No. 8 New York, 27-23, in the Eastern Conference standings.

The Knicks stunned the Heat by taking the best-of-5 series opener in Miami 95-75, but blew their chance to close out the series at home when Miami won Game 4 87-72. That set up a fifth and deciding game in Miami, and it went down to the wire. The Knicks trailed by three before an offensive rebound and two free throws by Ewing made it 77-76 Miami, then Sprewell stripped the ball from Heat point guard Tim Hardaway with 24.9 seconds left to give the Knicks another chance.

After a timeout, they ran a play for Sprewell, but Terry Porter kept him away from the basket and the Knicks were in disarray when the ball was knocked out of bounds by Porter with 4.5 seconds left. Houston caught the inbounds pass above the key, took two dribbles and then lofted an awkward, one-handed runner over Mourning's outstretched arm that hit the front of the rim, bounded high off the backboard and nestled through the net with :00.8 on the clock, giving New York a 78-77 upset and making the Knicks the second eighth seed to knock a No. 1 from the playoffs.

WHEN SECONDS COUNT

This is what it's all about. Here is Christian Laettner's game-winning shot in overtime that carried Duke past Kentucky, 104-103, in the 1992 NCAA East Finals. Duke went on to win the National Championship that year.

Arizona's Miles Simon holds the ball over his head after Arizona beat Kentucky 84-79, to win the 1997 National Championship.

AP/Wide World Photos

WHEN SECONDS COUNT

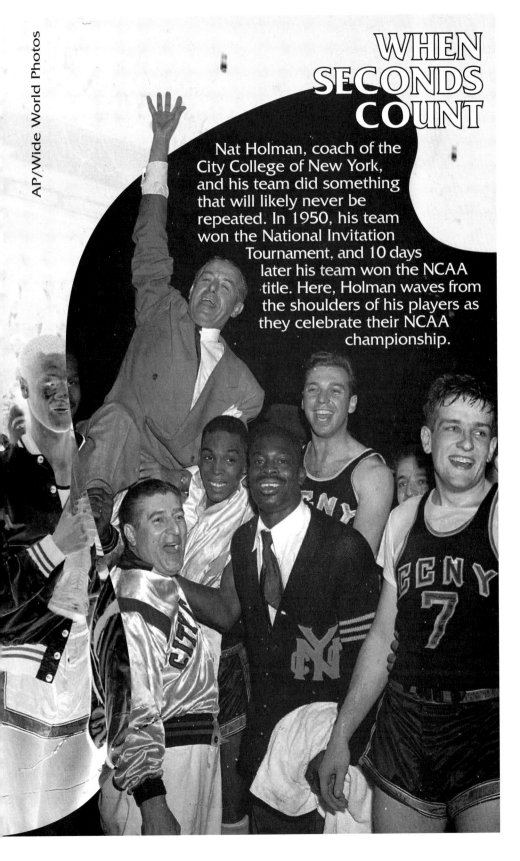

WHEN SECONDS COUNT

Nat Holman, coach of the City College of New York, and his team did something that will likely never be repeated. In 1950, his team won the National Invitation Tournament, and 10 days later his team won the NCAA title. Here, Holman waves from the shoulders of his players as they celebrate their NCAA championship.

This team from Milan High School shocked the basketball-crazy state of Indiana when it became the last small school to win the state's single-class state championship in 1954. In 1996, the Indiana High School Athletic Association replaced the single-class system with a system of tournaments based on school enrollment.

AP/Wide World Photos

WHEN
SECONDS
COUNT

WHEN SECONDS COUNT

Lisa Leslie scored 101 points in the first half of a game for Morningside High School in Los Angeles in 1990. The opposing team, South Torrance High, prevented Leslie from breaking Cheryl Miller's record of 104 points in a game by not playing the second half of the game.

Wilt Chamberlain of the Philadelphia Warriors set an NBA record by scoring 100 points in a 169-147 victory over the New York Knickerbockers on March 2, 1962.

WHEN SECONDS COUNT

WHEN SECONDS COUNT

Larry Bird celebrates The Celtics' last-second victory over the Detroit Pistons in Game 5 of the 1987 NBA Playoffs.

When he was done after his game-winning shot in Game 5 of the 1998 NBA Finals, Michael Jordan had earned six NBA championships, won a record 72 games in the 1995-1996 season, captured 10 scoring titles and was named NBA MVP five times and Finals MVP six times.

WHEN SECONDS COUNT

"If it hits an inch to the right, it falls off right," said Knicks veteran Herb Williams. "If it hits an inch to the left, it falls off left. But it just kissed that sucker perfectly."

"It sent chills up my spine," said Knicks point guard Charlie Ward. "We got the good roll today."

"It was," said Houston, "the biggest shot of my life."

After sweeping an injury-riddled Atlanta Hawks team, the Knicks met another arch-rival, the Indiana Pacers, in the Eastern Conference Finals. Again, there was a history between these two teams, with the Pacers, in general, and guard Reggie Miller, in particular, having gotten under the Knicks' skin more than once in the 1990s.

But the Knicks had another miracle finish in their bag of tricks. It came at the end of Game 3, after the teams had split the first two games in Indianapolis. The Pacers led 91-88 with 11.9 seconds remaining, New York ball at mid-court. The inbounds pass came to forward Larry Johnson, who squared off against Antonio Davis of the Pacers. Johnson used a head fake, then made a quick move that got Davis off balance and reaching at Johnson's waist. Johnson went up with his three-pointer, it went through to tie the score with 5.7 seconds left—and the referee's whistle sounded, signaling a touch foul against Davis. Johnson stepped to the line, hit the free throw to complete the four-point play, and New York had a 92-91 victory.

"That was the biggest shot of my life. I think in high school I can remember making one or two (game-winners), and it was a big thing in high school, but nothing bigger than this," said Johnson. "When you hit it, it doesn't sink in right away. Then it's like, 'Oh, my!' And there's Spike Lee coming at you, and the whole Garden crowd. Wow!"

"I thought I'd seen a lot of things," said Indiana's Miller. "We had a three-point lead, and you think the worst thing you can do is tie. I was wrong. I'm usually on the other side of shots like that!"

"First time I've ever seen a four-point play decide a game," said Knicks coach Van Gundy. "That was a miracle."

The Knicks went on to beat the Pacers in six games and advance to the NBA Finals, but that's where they ran out of miracles. Facing the San Antonio Spurs and their Twin Towers, Tim Duncan and David Robinson, and with their own center, Ewing, sidelined by a foot injury, the Knicks were simply outsized and overmatched. The Spurs won the series in five games to capture their first-ever NBA championship. But for the Knicks, just getting to the NBA Finals after they had been stalled at .500 in early April was a miracle finish in itself.

00:27

• •

Slick Leonard Lifts Indiana over Kansas

"HOW are we ever going to beat this team?" Indiana guard and team captain Bobby Leonard asked his backcourt mate, Burke Scott, as they watched Kansas use a ferocious full-court press to come up with 21 steals in a 79-53 dismantling of favored Washington in the semifinals of the 1953 NCAA championship.

The Hoosiers found a way, and Leonard played a key role. His free throw with 27 seconds left gave Indiana a 69-68 victory and the national crown—ironically, over the very same team it had beaten 13 years earlier for the 1940 title.

Indiana entered the NCAA tournament with just three losses, all on buzzer-beaters, but almost got knocked off in the first round before pulling out an 82-80 decision over DePaul. Then the Hoosiers avenged one of their three defeats, and did so in style, pounding Notre Dame 79-66 as 6-9 center Don Schlundt set a Chicago Stadium scoring record with 41 points (remember, this is 1953—Michael Jordan wasn't even born yet).

The national semifinal between Indiana and Louisiana State shaped up as a duel between Schlundt and the Tigers' 6-9 star, future Hall of Famer Bob Pettit. But while those two were battling inside, Leonard had the hot hand from outside and tallied 22 points in the Hoosiers' 80-67 victory.

The title game was remarkably close throughout. Kansas held the biggest lead of the game at 39-33 in the first half. But Branch McCracken put Schlundt, who had been on the bench with three personal fouls, back into the game and he sparked an 8-2 Indiana run that produced a 41-41 tie at halftime.

The intensity only picked up in the second half. There was a dispute when Kansas's B.H. Born was whistled for a foul midway through the period. The scorers said it was his fifth foul, but Kansas coach Phog Allen ran to the table and claimed the team's own book showed Born with just four. The officials checked and finally agreed with Allen, permitting Born to stay in the game and enraging McCracken, who said, "Born should be out. We're your guest and you're robbing us."

Born finally did foul out later in the half, by which time both Schlundt and Leonard had picked up technical fouls for disputing officials' calls. Then, with Indiana leading 68-65 late in the game, forward Charles Kraak was called for a foul, angrily slammed the ball and was assessed yet another technical. That meant three free throws for Kansas—a chance to tie the game from the foul line—plus possession of the ball.

Kansas junior Hal Patterson made one of the two personals, then Al Kelley missed the technical, leaving Indiana up by two. But on the ensuing possession, Dean Kelley, Al's brother, scored on a drive to tie the score at 68-68 with 65 seconds remaining.

Indiana planned to hold the ball for the last shot, but with 27 seconds left, Dean Kelley bumped Leonard and was called for a foul. Leonard missed his first free-throw attempt and then Allen called a timeout to try to ice him, to let him think about his miss and hopefully get him jittery about the second try.

But Leonard, who later went on to a solid professional career before serving as head coach and broadcaster for the Indiana Pacers in the ABA and NBA, wasn't nicknamed "Slick" for nothing. After the teams were whistled back onto the court, he stepped up to the line and calmly knocked down the free throw for a 69-68 lead. "I had been to the line under pressure so much all season," he said later.

Kansas still had plenty of time, plus the ball. Allen ordered his team to run some time off the clock and then set up Al Kelley for a jumper with about five seconds left. If it went in, they'd have the lead; if he was fouled, he'd go to the line to shoot for a tie or the lead; and if he missed, there would be a couple of seconds left for a possible offensive rebound.

Indiana's defense, however, would not let it happen that way. By the time the clock ticked down to five seconds, Kelley was surrounded by defenders. So he passed the ball to Jerry Alberts, a seldom-used reserve playing in place of Born. Alberts didn't particularly want to take the shot from the corner, but with time running down, he was left with little choice.

Leonard, remembering how Indiana had suffered its three losses under similar circumstances, held his breath as Alberts' shot arched toward the basket.

"I thought, 'Please don't let this go through,'" he recalled.

He got his wish. It bounced off the rim, Indiana got the rebound and time ran out, giving the Hoosiers the national championship. Schlundt was Indiana's leading scorer with 30 points, but it was Leonard's free throw that provided the margin of victory.

Afterward, McCracken told reporters that his team captain "had ice water in his veins." When told of that remark, Leonard smiled and said, "If that was ice water, it sure felt warm to me."

00:26

• •

Hoosier Hysteria: Bailey Leads Bedford to State Title

High school basketball is something special in Indiana, where schoolboy hoops are taken most seriously. Hoosier Hysteria is the term used to describe the spirited support shown by small towns and big cities alike for their high school teams as they compete in the statewide tournament for a spot in the final four in Indianapolis.

In fact, when the state decided in 1996 to go away from its traditional one-class tournament open to all schools in favor of multiple tournaments so schools could compete against others of comparable enrollment, it provoked a storm of controversy far beyond anything that could be imagined in other states.

Many players have flourished in the Indiana schoolboy ranks, from John Wooden to Clyde Lovellette to Oscar Robertson to Rick Mount to George McGinnis to Larry Bird to Steve Alford. But none scored as many points in his high school career as Damon Bailey of Bedford North Lawrence. Bailey, the state's "Mr. Basketball" in 1990, scored 3,134 points in 110 games, erasing the 29-year-old record of 3,019 points set by Marion Pierce of Lewisville.

Bailey finished his schoolboy career with a flourish, tallying 30 points as Bedford North Lawrence defeated previously undefeated Concord 63-60 in the state championship game. But that was just the tip of the iceberg.

The game was played before a sellout crowd of 41,046 at the Hoosier Dome in Indianapolis, the most ever to see a high school contest, as the tournament made its first appearance in the dome after having been played at Butler Fieldhouse and Market Square Arena. And Bailey scored his team's last 11 points in the final 2:38 to overcome a six-point deficit and turn defeat into victory.

"When we were down six, Damon just kind of took over," said Bedford coach Dan Bush. "We wanted to get him the ball. We knew he'd create something good for himself or for somebody else, and he got it done. That's why he's the best player in the country."

Indeed, Bailey drew national acclaim during his career at Bedford. He was cited in *Sports Illustrated* and on ESPN, and reporters from cities like Los Angeles, Philadelphia, Detroit and Chicago found their way to Bedford to see the schoolboy phenom.

Bush was once asked to pick Bailey's best games at Bedford, but demurred. "It would be hard to do, because he had so many good ones," the coach said.

Bailey averaged 28.5 points per game in his high school career, scoring in double figures in all 110 games and tallying a high of 51 points against Jeffersonville in his sophomore year. His season averages were 23.6, 27.4, 27.2 and 31.4 ppg as he helped Bedford to a 99-11 record in his four years. Bedford was 40-0 on its home floor during Bailey's time there, and the 6,300-seat gym was sold out for every game. "It was rumored that tickets got to be a big thing in some divorces," wrote Bob Williams in his book, *Hoosier Hysteria.*

Bailey led his team to the final four of the state tournament three times, getting 20 points in a 70-61 loss to Marion as a freshman and 25 points (plus 10 rebounds) in a 60-53 loss to Muncie Central as a sophomore. Those only set the stage for his dramatic finale, as Bailey personally carried Bedford from a 58-52 deficit to a 63-60 victory and the 1990 state title with a pair of baskets and seven free throws.

Selected prep Player of the Decade by The Associated Press and *Parade* magazine, Bailey went on to play college ball for Bobby Knight at Indiana University, where he had a solid career but did not dominate the sport the way he had in high school. He averaged 19.6 points and 4.3 assists per game as a senior, when he was named to the All-Big Ten team and Third Team All-America. He finished his career as Indiana's fifth-leading scorer and tied for second in assists, as well as the school's all-time leader in three-pointers.

Bailey, who suffered knee injuries in college and never made his mark in the NBA, was constantly under a microscope at Indiana after his schoolboy heroics.

"Think for just a second how hard it might be to be an 18-year-old kid named Damon Bailey," said Knight. "I don't think there's anybody who has ever, as an 18-year-old or a 40-year-old, been in quite the position Damon Bailey was in when he came to Indiana. For four years I've probably been Bailey's biggest critic, but I also think for four years I've probably been his biggest fan."

00:25

●●●●●●●●●●●●●●●●●●●●●●●●●

Larry Bird and Magic Johnson: A Rivalry for All Time

They came from different backgrounds but shared a love of the game and an appreciation for how it should be played. They understood that basketball was, above all else, a team sport, one where five players with five egos must learn to share one basketball and develop a greater team ego if the team is to succeed.

"Basketball is a game where no one player is more important than the team," said Earvin "Magic" Johnson. "Both of us want to bring out the best in our teammates. We think the same way about the game," said Larry Bird.

Together, Bird and Johnson revived the sport, first on the college level with their brilliant 1979 seasons culminating in their showdown at the NCAA title game, then for more than a decade as professionals with two of the NBA's most storied franchises, the Boston Celtics and Los Angeles Lakers. To cap it off, they served together as honorary captains of the original Dream Team that won the gold medal for the United States at the 1992 Olympics in Barcelona, a team that captured the imagination of sports fans around the world and really opened up the sport to a global audience.

Though best known as consummate team players, each was brilliant individually, too.

Bird was an uncanny shooter with supreme self-confidence, a guy who once walked into the locker room at one of the NBA's three-point shootouts and told his rivals, "Okay, which one of you guys is going to finish second?" Ultra-competitive, as so many great players are, there was no one else you'd rather have to attempt a last shot with the game on the line. He also was a solid rebounder, averaging 10 per game as a pro; a canny team defender who became the Celtics' all-time leader in steals; and an outstanding passer with an acute court sense, to the point that he always knew where the other nine players were on the floor, and seemed to know where they were going before they figured it out themselves.

Johnson was a fancy passer, but he was no passing fancy. There was every bit as much substance as sizzle to his game. When he had to, he could dominate by scoring or rebounding—as evidence, consider the 42 points and 15 rebounds he came up with as a rookie while filling in for injured center Kareem Abdul-Jabbar in the last game of the 1980 NBA Finals, giving the Lakers their first of five championships in the '80s. But it was his dazzling ballhandling that most distinguished his game and stamped the Lakers' offense as "Showtime." Nothing revved up the celebrity-studded crowd at the Forum more than Johnson in the middle of the fast break, pushing the ball up the floor, faking defenders out of position and then slipping no-look passes to the likes of Norm Nixon, Byron Scott, Michael Cooper, Jamaal Wilkes and James Worthy on the wing, or laying it off to a trailer like Kareem Abdul-Jabbar.

Off the court, Bird and Johnson came to national attention as polar opposites. Bird was the introvert, the shy farm boy from Indiana who distrusted strangers, wanted little to do with the trappings of celebrity and was quickly taken to heart by the blue-collar fans of Boston, who embraced his work ethic. Johnson was an extrovert, an outgoing kid from the streets of Lansing, Michigan, whose smile could light up a room and who could not have landed in a more perfect professional home than Tinseltown, a place that recognizes and appreciates star quality perhaps more than any other.

They did not become friends until a few years into their pro careers, when Johnson went to Bird's hometown of French Lick, Indiana, to shoot a commercial together for Converse, the sneaker they both endorsed at the time. "We messed around that day," said Bird. "I got him to drive the four-wheeler around and he had never done anything like that before. Our relationship really blossomed that day because it was the first time we had ever really sat down and talked. If we had grown up together or if we were teammates, I think we'd have been best friends." Johnson came away from the commercial shoot feeling much the same, and the admiration they each had expressed for the other's on-court skills blossomed into a warm and lasting friendship that grew with their careers.

Bird and Johnson met in one of the most significant games in college basketball history, the 1979 NCAA championship game in Salt Lake City that attracted major media attention because of the two superstars and raised the sport's public profile. "The buildup for the game was crazy," recalled Bird. "The press attention was enormous. The idea of the two of us playing for the NCAA title had captured everyone's imagination."

Bird, who had been drafted by Boston a year earlier but elected to remain in school for his final season of eligibility (he sat out one year as a transfer student), had led little-known Indiana State to an unbeaten record going into the title game against Michigan State. The Spartans, with Johnson in his sophomore year playing along with future NBA frontcourt men Greg Kelser and Jay Vincent, had lost six games, including five in the Big Ten. But they had gotten better as the season wore on and were peaking in postseason.

Bird, who shot 16-for-19 and scored 35 in the national semi-finals against DePaul, seemed to be hampered by a sore thumb against Michigan State, though he refused to use it as an excuse for his 7-

for-21 shooting. Nonetheless, said Vincent, "I never saw him so far off. He shot two over the basket." Bird also was frustrated by the Spartans' zone defense that strung Johnson, Vincent and Kelser, three future NBA first-round draft picks, along the baseline and put two men on Bird whenever he touched the ball. "We thought we had proved that we could beat every kind of defense, but we had never seen anything like that zone of theirs," said Bird. "I couldn't do anything at all against it. They did a really good job on me."

Michigan State jumped out to a 37-28 lead and stretched it to 50-34 early in the second half. Indiana State pulled within six with 10:10 left, but that was as close as the Sycamores would come. Johnson scored seven of his game-high 24 points in the next five minutes and Michigan State pulled away to a 75-64 victory and the NCAA title. Bird finished with 19 points.

"What impressed me most about Larry came near the end, when we were celebrating," said Johnson. "He had his head in a towel, crying. Losing really hurt him, and that's the sign of a true competitor."

Both players had an immediate impact upon joining the NBA, a league that in 1979 was sorely in need of help both in terms of the way the game was played on the court and the way players conducted themselves off the court. Bird won Rookie of the Year honors in 1979-80, but Johnson led the Lakers to the NBA championship and gained NBA Finals MVP. It was the start of a great rivalry that would see one team, or both, make the NBA Finals for 10 straight seasons. More important, the team-oriented, selfless style of play both Bird and Johnson exemplified, as well as their strong work ethic and intense competitiveness, served to silence the many critics who had contended that pro basketball players were lazy, overpaid athletes who cared only about their own scoring totals.

"I fear no one except Larry Bird," Johnson once said, "because if they keep it close and he has a chance to win it, well, he's going to win that game. He just knows how to win. He wants to win and he will do anything to win. That man knows how to play the game of basketball."

"I have always admired the way Magic handles himself," said Bird. "I feel he's the greatest all-around team player in basketball. I have always looked up to him because he knows how to win. Magic plays basketball the way I think you should play the game."

Basketball has had many great rivalries, such as Wilt Chamberlain vs. Bill Russell, Oscar Robertson vs. Jerry West, and before them, George Mikan vs. Bob Kurland. But the rivalry between Larry Bird and Magic Johnson, coming when it did, laid the foundation for the Michael Jordan era and helped turn America's game into a global fascination.

00:24

The Shot Clock That Saved the NBA

Pro basketball in the 1950s bore little resemblance to the fast-paced, acrobatic game on display nightly in today's NBA arenas. All too often the game was played at a snail's pace, with one team opening up a lead and freezing the ball until time ran out. The only thing the trailing team could do was foul, and games became foul-shooting contests.

"That was the way the game was played—get a lead and put the ball in the icebox," said Bob Cousy of the Boston Celtics, nicknamed the Houdini of the Hardwood for his magical ballhandling skill. "Teams literally started sitting on the ball in the third quarter. Coaches are conservative by nature, and it didn't make much sense to play a wide-open game. We'd get a lead, and you'd see good ol' No. 14 doing his tricks out there."

If not good ol' No. 14, then it would be one of the other premier guards of that era, such as Dick McGuire, Slater Martin, Bob Davies or Andy Phillip, who would dribble until they were fouled, and the parade from one free-throw line to the other would begin.

"The game had become a stalling game," said Danny Biasone, owner of the NBA's Syracuse Nationals, who in 1963 moved to Philadelphia and were renamed the 76ers. "A team would get ahead, even in the first half, and it would go into a stall. The other team would keep fouling, and it got to be a constant parade to the foul line. In 1952 we played a game in which neither team took a shot in the last eight minutes. It was a parade between foul lines, and, boy, was it dull!"

Dull was the last thing NBA moguls wanted when the league was still in its infancy, struggling for a place on the American sports scene, but dull was what the league was becoming. On November 22, 1950, the Fort Wayne Pistons edged the Minneapolis Lakers 19-18 in the lowest-scoring game in NBA annals, one in which the teams scored only four baskets apiece in the entire game. Three years later, 107 fouls were called and 130 free throws shot in a playoff game between Boston and Syracuse, one in which Cousy scored 30 of his then-record 50 points on free throws. In 1954, Syracuse beat New York 75-69 in another playoff horror show in which free throws outnumbered baskets 75-34.

"If you're a promoter, that won't do. You've got to have offense, because offense excites people," said Biasone.

Clearly, something had to be done to perk up the game if the NBA was to attract fans and survive. In 1953 the league began awarding two free throws instead of one for a backcourt foul, but teams got around that penalty by waiting till the ball passed the mid-court line before fouling. Something more drastic was called for.

"We needed a time element in our game," said Biasone. "There was no way we could stop the stalling and fouling without a time element. Other sports had limits—in baseball you get three outs to score, in football you must make 10 yards in four downs or you lose the ball. But in basketball, if you had the lead and a good ball handler, you could play around all night. The only way for the other team to stop that was to grab him and send him to the foul line. Then you'd foul him back. It was dull.

"After the 1953-54 season, I got 10 players together in Syracuse and tried out my idea with a stopwatch in a little scrimmage game. The Board of Governors agreed to try it out in the exhibition season, and after that they voted it in for the regular season.

"Pro basketball would not have survived without a clock."

Biasone's idea was a shot clock, giving a team 24 seconds in which to attempt a shot or else lose possession of the ball. To deal with the matter of excessive fouling, the Board of Governors also adopted a rule limiting the number of fouls per team per quarter, after which each foul became a shooting foul. The two rules complemented each other perfectly.

The 24-second shot clock made its debut on October 30, 1954, and had an immediate impact, as the Rochester Royals beat the Boston Celtics 98-95 in what would have been the seventh-highest-scoring game of the previous season. During 1954-55, the first season with the 24-second clock, NBA teams averaged 93.1 points per game, an increase of 13.6 ppg over the year before—and 10.5 of the extra points came from the field, with only 3.1 from the foul line. In 1955 the Boston Celtics became the first team in NBA history to average over 100 points per game for an entire season, and four years later every team was doing it.

Cousy, whose career spanned the time before and after the shot clock was introduced, recognized its value immediately.

"Before the new rule, the last quarter could be deadly," he said. "With the clock, we had constant action. I think it saved the NBA at that time. It allowed the game to breathe and progress."

"It was the single most important rule change in the last 50 years," said longtime Boston Celtics coach and executive Red Auerbach.

"The whole purpose of the 24-second rule—to make the game fast and furious, with plenty of action—was accomplished," said Eddie Gottlieb, one of the founders of the NBA who owned and coached the Philadelphia Warriors when the rule was put into effect.

How did Biasone come up with the unusual number of 24 seconds for his time limit? Why not one minute, or 30 seconds, or some other round number?

"The number of seconds wasn't that important, as long as we had the time element," said Biasone, who then explained that he and his general manager, Leo Ferris, worked out the formula this way: "By taking the average number of shots two teams would take during a game, which was about 120, and dividing that into the length of a game, which was 48 minutes, or 2,880 seconds, you come up with 24. But it could have been anything—just so there was some kind of a time limit."

Coincidentally (or not), Biasone's Syracuse Nats won the NBA title in 1954-55, the first year of the shot clock. And they did it by rallying from a 17-point deficit to beat Fort Wayne 92-91 in the seventh game of the championship series.

Said Biasone, "If it wasn't for the shot clock, it would have been the dullest game in history. Fort Wayne was up by 17, and under the old rules, they would have gone into a stall. Then there'd have been a flurry of fouls. Everyone kidded me that I thought of the clock just to win the championship, but that wasn't so. I just wanted to see a whole game."

"The adoption of the clock was the most important event in the NBA," said the late Maurice Podoloff, the NBA's first commissioner.

College basketball remained without a shot clock until the 1980s, when various conferences began experimenting with clocks of different lengths. The NCAA adopted a 45-second shot clock for the 1985-86 season and reduced the amount of time to 35 seconds beginning with the 1993-94 college season. A 30-second shot clock is used in the WNBA and in global competitions sponsored by FIBA, the International Basketball Federation, and the Olympics and World Championships.

00:23

. . . .

Jordan Hits "The Shot"

In Chicago and Cleveland it is known simply as "The Shot," and it changed the courses of two franchises.

Michael Jordan's last-second jumper against the Cleveland Cavaliers gave the Chicago Bulls a 101-100 victory in the deciding Game 5 of their 1989 first-round playoff series. That shot, and

Jordan's subsequent leaping, fist-pumping celebration, became a symbol for pro basketball as it headed into the 1990s, thanks to seemingly endless television replays. It had everything the sport's marketers could ask for: excitement, grace, athleticism, refined skill and raw emotion, as well as the world's most popular and charismatic athlete.

The Bulls were still trying to discover the formula for success in 1989. They had won 50 games the year before, after six straight losing seasons, but had been soundly beaten by Detroit in the second round of the playoffs. Power forward Charles Oakley had been traded to New York for center Bill Cartwright, and youngsters Scottie Pippen and Horace Grant were given more prominent roles in support of Jordan, the league's leading scorer for the third year in a row. The result was a respectable 47-35 record that left the Bulls fifth in the powerful Central Division, 16 games behind the Pistons.

The Cleveland Cavaliers, meanwhile, had assembled one of the NBA's finest young teams. Their center was Brad Daugherty, the top overall pick of the 1986 NBA Draft, a smooth passer and capable scorer. Mark Price and Ron Harper, completing their third seasons, formed one of the most explosive backcourts in the league, averaging over 18 points per game apiece.

Small forward Larry Nance was anything but small at 6-foot-10, a fine rebounder and shot blocker who leaped well enough to win the slam-dunk contest, was good for 15-20 points a game, and made the All-Defensive First Team to boot. Steady Mike Sanders shared the other frontcourt spot with the explosive John "Hot Rod" Williams, giving Cleveland different looks at the position while combining for nearly 21 points and 10 rebounds a game.

This group had been together for a couple of seasons and, under the guidance of Lenny Wilkens, set a franchise record by winning 57 games in 1988-89. The Cavs were a team on the rise, a team with championship aspirations.

The playoffs pitted Cleveland against Chicago in a first-round rematch of their series from 1988, when Chicago won the deciding Game 5 107-101. This time, however, Cleveland had the home-court advantage as a result of having finished 10 games ahead of the Bulls in the regular season. What's more, the Cavs had beaten the Bulls six straight times during the regular season. Nonetheless, before the playoffs, Jordan brashly predicted that Chicago would win the series.

Chicago stole that home-court advantage by winning the opening game of the best-of-5 series in Cleveland 95-88. But after each team won a home game, the Bulls turned the advantage back over to Cleveland by failing to close out the Cavs in Game 4, dropping a 108-105 overtime decision.

Momentum seemed to be on Cleveland's side as it headed back to the Coliseum in Richfield, Ohio, where the Cavs had compiled a 37-4 record during the regular season, including 22 wins in a row. It seemed unlikely that Cleveland would lose twice on its home floor in a span of 10 days.

The game was tight from start to finish, coming down to a spectacular final play. With three seconds left on the clock, Cleveland held a 100-99 lead, but Chicago had the ball following a timeout.

The Bulls set up to inbound the ball from mid-court on the right sideline. The Cavs knew Chicago would try to get the ball into Jordan's hands right away, so they set up a double-team, with Nance joining Craig Ehlo, their best defensive guard, to try to deny him the ball. Jordan came out from the lane, running directly at Nance, then cut to his left and took the inbounds pass near the right sideline, above the top of the circle.

He took one dribble to his left, then another, moving into the key just above the foul line. Nance was behind him and out of the play, while Ehlo was struggling to keep pace. What happened next is perhaps the ultimate example of hang time. Jordan went up for his jump shot while gliding slightly to his left, and Ehlo cut in front of him from right to left and made a running leap to attempt a block, his hand in Jordan's face. Jordan seemed to hang suspended in midair, his right hand under the ball in shooting position, his left hand on its side to guide it, as Ehlo reached the apex of his leap and then sailed past him on the way down. It was only once Ehlo had hit the floor that Jordan, on his way down but still at least a foot off the floor, released his shot. The 16-footer went through at the buzzer. When he landed, Jordan pumped his fist in celebration and leaped into the air once again, a reaction that was caught by the national TV cameras and replayed again and again.

"I put my credibility on the line by predicting we would win. I had to make the shot," said Jordan. "There's nothing like it in the world, that feeling of having the ball in the final seconds as the clock slowly ticks off, going up and hanging in the air and then hitting the shot. Man, that is total control. There's just no other feeling like it. None."

Following the 101-100 victory, Chicago beat New York in six games to advance to the Eastern Conference Finals, where they were ousted by the Detroit Pistons in six. Beating the Cavaliers for the second year in a row, and this time by taking the decisive game on the road, was an important step in the team's growth into a champion. Two years later they would win the first of their six championships in the 1990s.

Cleveland, meanwhile, has never been the same after losing Game 5 to the Bulls for the second year in a row. The Cavs dipped to 42-40 in 1989-90, a drop of 15 games, and once again were unable to get out of the first round of the playoffs, this time bowing to Philadelphia in five games. Cleveland failed to make the playoffs in 1990-91, has a 14-26 record in its postseason appearances since then and has yet to reach the NBA Finals.

00:22

• •

Armstrong Weaves
His Magic

It was the kind of play that requires athleticism, basketball instinct and a never-say-die attitude, and Darrell Armstrong has them all. Especially the latter.

"He never quits," said Orlando Magic teammate Ike Austin. "He's got a big heart. And when you've got a big heart, you can do anything you want."

On March 15, 1999, Armstrong spent the better part of 48 minutes chasing Philadelphia's explosive guard, Allen Iverson, around the Orlando Arena floor. The lightning-quick, 6-foot-1 Armstrong had done a masterful job, holding the man who would go on to win the NBA scoring championship to 14 points, barely half his season's average.

But with 3.3 seconds left in the game, it looked like his effort would be for naught. The Magic trailed 73-72 and Philadelphia had possession of the ball out of bounds at mid-court. All the Sixers needed to secure the victory was inbound the ball and run out the clock.

George Lynch looked to throw the ball in, couldn't find anyone and called a timeout. On his next attempt, Lynch tried to force a pass into a group of teammates that included Iverson, Eric Snow and Aaron McKie. Armstrong, who was guarding Iverson, made a fake toward Snow, then stepped back in front of Iverson and got his hands on the pass. He deflected it toward the Orlando basket, caught up with the ball and dribbled in for a layup at the buzzer, giving the Magic a 74-73 victory.

"Darrell Armstrong made one of the biggest plays this franchise has ever seen," said Magic forward Horace Grant. "This just goes to show, you have to play 48 minutes in this league—47 and change doesn't get it done. We came into the locker room and we were looking for the champagne to pop. That's how we felt."

"I was shocked when I saw the ball coming. My eyes just got real wide," said Armstrong. "I put the ball in front of me and just took off. I knew I had enough time, but not by much."

"We literally stole one tonight," said Orlando's coach, Hall of Famer Chuck Daly. "Darrell Armstrong just has a heart bigger than his chest."

He's needed it, for while some athletes seem destined for greatness and the game's rewards almost from birth, Armstrong has had to hustle and scramble for everything he's gotten.

In 1991 he was out of the game, cooking yarn on the graveyard shift at the Dixie Yarn Mill back in North Carolina. In 1999 he won both the NBA's Sixth Man Award and Most Improved Player Award, climaxing one of basketball's most remarkable rags-to-riches stories. The five-year, $18 million contract he signed with the Magic on January 21, 1999, was the pot of gold at the end of the rainbow, the reward for having survived a long, circuitous journey that took Armstrong to places like Spain and Cyprus and saw him play in leagues with enough letters to fill a bowl of alphabet soup.

Armstrong grew up in Gastonia, North Carolina, where he was the place-kicker on the Ashbrook High School football team before finally trying out for basketball in his senior year. He went to nearby Fayetteville State, a Division II school, and after sitting out his freshman year, played three seasons and compiled career averages of 14.3 points, 3.9 rebounds and 3.8 assists per game. Those modest numbers belied his intensity, especially on defense; coach Jeff Capel frequently had to admonish Armstrong to let up on his teammates during practice rather than wear them out.

Not drafted by any NBA franchise, Armstrong was making $250 a week at the yarn factory when he turned to the South Georgia franchise of the Global Basketball Association. When that league folded out from under him, he played a couple of games for the Capital Region team in the Continental Basketball Association, then took his game overseas.

In 1993-94 he played for a team in Cyprus and averaged 32 points and eight assists per game in the Turkish League. In 1994-95 he was off to Spain, where he averaged 24.6 points and 4.5 assists for the Coren Orense team in the ACB, the Spanish League. That's how he spent his winters; summers were devoted to the United States Basketball League, where he played three seasons for the Atlanta Eagles.

While playing for Atlanta in the spring of 1994, Armstrong got his big break. John Gabriel, now the general manager of the Magic, went to scout a guard named Mark Bell of the USBL's Daytona Beach Hooters in a game against Armstrong's club. Armstrong outplayed Bell, and during a timeout late in the game, Gabriel invited him to attend the Magic's free agent camp. Although he spent that winter in Spain, Armstrong came home and finally signed with the Magic on April 8, 1995.

Leg injuries limited him to 41 minutes in 1995-96, but the following season he was healthy and appeared in 67 games, averaging 6.1 points. He played especially well in the playoffs against Miami, when injuries forced the shift of Penny Hardaway to shooting guard and Armstrong was given the chance to run the offense. He had 21 points and eight assists as the Magic staved off a sweep with a victory in Game 3, and 12 points and nine rebounds as they evened the series in Game 4 before bowing in Game 5. In 1997-98, with Hardaway limited to 19 games due to injury, playing time opened up for Armstrong and he took advantage of the opportunity, posting career highs in virtually every category until a torn rotator cuff ended his season after just 48 games.

But those two campaigns were enough to convince the Magic to open their checkbooks to keep Armstrong, and he repaid them with a brilliant season in 1998-99 when he averaged 13.8 points, 6.7 assists, 3.6 rebounds and 2.16 steals in 30 minutes per game. He ranked third in the league in free-throw percentage (.904), eighth in steals and 12th in assists.

The season had many highlights, including 19 fourth-quarter points in a 94-87 triumph over Miami on March 28; a career-high 28 points in a win over Charlotte on March 23, a mark he would later tie in a victory over the Boston Celtics on April 5; a game-winning 17-foot jumper in an 88-87 victory over Indiana on April 27; and 27 points and nine assists in a 93-86 win over Washington on April 28.

The steal and game-winning driving layup against Philadelphia, however, gives a more complete picture of Armstrong's value to the Magic. It was a play that enabled Orlando to win a game despite shooting just 28.6 percent from the field, lowest in franchise history, and despite being outrebounded 58-48. Because besides his statistics, which on that night showed 14 points and six assists, Armstrong is an outstanding defender capable of stopping an opponent one-on-one or taking an opposing team out of its rhythm. And his perseverance and work ethic are an inspiration for teammates.

"I love people with passion, and he is as passionate about the game as any person you'll ever find," said broadcaster Doug Collins, a former NBA player and head coach. "He brings you energy. He brings you life on the floor all the time."

"You've got to love his attitude and the way he plays," added Daly. "Those kind of people come along in your career very infrequently, and I'm happy for him."

00:21

● ●

Bradley, Russell Duel at Madison Square Garden

College basketball was still largely a campus-based sport in the mid-1960s, with all but a select few games played in college gyms and the NCAA Final Four yet to explode into an event of global proportion. Even the midwinter holiday tournaments, which today are so common, were few and far between, so that each stood out as a significant event.

One of the foremost was the ECAC Holiday Festival, which was played each year at New York's Madison Square Garden. Invitations to this tournament were precious, because in the pre-cable days, when national television appearances were rare, schools considered the lure of a holiday trip to the Garden and the media mecca of New York to be a major attraction when it came to recruiting prospects, as well as showcasing their programs for prospective alumni donors. Instead of losing teams to the many warm-weather sites that host tournaments today, the people who ran the Holiday Festival had their pick of the top teams and brightest stars in the land.

That's what they had in 1964, when the field included two 6-foot-5 forwards who would earn All-America status and lead their schools to national prominence: Bill Bradley of Princeton, a senior, and Cazzie Russell of Michigan, a junior.

Both were terrific college players who excelled at virtually every aspect of the game. Bradley might have been a bit better as a pure long-range shooter, while Russell was a tad quicker and more explosive going to the basket, but really that was splitting hairs. Both were outstanding offensive players who managed to be productive despite regularly being double-teamed or running up against zones designed to keep them in check. Together, they brought star power and excitement to the Garden and created a buzz for the Holiday Festival in particular and college basketball in general.

Their teams had very different personalities. Princeton played a patient, ball-control offense (though not quite as patient as it later would under Pete Carril; the Tigers in 1965 were coached by Butch van Breda Kolff, who later coached in the NBA and was not so reticent to run) and a stingy defense, working to control the tempo of the game, make every shot count and allow no easy baskets. Michigan liked to run at every opportunity and was willing to trade baskets, relying on its talent and athleticism to wear down opponents in a fast-breaking, wide-open style of play.

As if to spotlight their showdown, each of the stars scored 36 points in the first round of the Holiday Festival, as Princeton beat Syracuse 77-67 and Michigan defeated Manhattan 90-77. More than 18,000 filled the old Madison Square Garden, on Eighth Avenue between 49th and 50th streets on the west side of Manhattan, for the Bradley-Russell duel.

Bradley was brilliant from the opening tip as Michigan tried, and failed, to play him straight up. He was all over the court, posting up, shooting from outside, driving to the basket, passing to open teammates on the rare occasions when he was denied his shot. He tallied more than half his team's points in the first half, outscoring Russell 23-8 in the opening 20 minutes. Michigan's stronger supporting cast, which included future pros Bill Buntin and Oliver

Darden, picked up most of the slack, however, and the Wolverines trailed by just 39-37 at halftime.

Michigan went to a full-court press following intermission in an effort to rattle Princeton and keep the ball out of Bradley's hands, or at least keep him from getting it when and where he wanted it within the Tigers' offense. It proved to be of little or no impact, as Bradley scored 18 more points, enabling Princeton to stretch its lead to 13 points at 76-63 with less than five minutes left in the game.

That's when disaster struck the Tigers, the roof caved in, or whatever other cliché you want to use. Bradley was whistled for his fifth personal foul with 4:37 remaining and left the game with 41 points, receiving a standing ovation from the sellout crowd.

Suddenly, the Tigers became a wheel without a hub. Lacking their star, they wilted under the pressure applied by the Wolverines in the stretch run. Russell, meanwhile, had saved his best for last. Princeton's 13-point lead disappeared in a flash, as Michigan reeled off 10 consecutive points, six of them by Russell. Not long after that, Russell scored on a three-point play and the game was tied 78-78. Everything Princeton had built in 35 minutes had been torn down in less than four by the Wolverines, as Bradley watched helplessly from the bench.

A missed shot by Princeton gave the ball back to Michigan in the final minute, and the Wolverines opted to hold it for the last shot. By now Russell was on fire, and there seemed little doubt he'd be the designated shooter. Sure enough, once it got under 10 seconds, Russell shook himself free and put up a 15-foot jumper that went in with three seconds left on the Garden clock, and Michigan had an 80-78 victory after outscoring Princeton 17-4 following Bradley's disqualification. Russell finished the game with 27 points, 11 of them in the final 4:37.

Bradley had won the battle between the two All-Americans, but Michigan had won the war. The two teams would meet again in the NCAA Final Four, and this time the Wolverines' victory was by a more decisive 93-76 margin. Again, Bradley won the individual battle, scoring 29 points before fouling out with six minutes to go while Russell scored 28; but once again, Michigan won the war.

The two stars would be reunited as professionals and would help the New York Knicks win the 1970 NBA championship, Bradley supplanting Russell in the Knicks' starting lineup, while the former Michigan star became a valuable sixth man. Bradley, who joined the Knicks in 1967-68 after two years in England on a Rhodes Scholarship, played his entire 10-year NBA career in New York. Russell, the Knicks' first-round pick in 1966, played five seasons with New York and then seven more with Golden State, Los Angeles and Chicago.

00:20

• •

Bird vs. Wilkins: Shootout in Boston Garden

"It was like two gunfighters waiting to blink," Hall of Famer Kevin McHale says of the 1988 playoff shootout in Boston Garden between Larry Bird and Dominique Wilkins. "I tell you, there was one stretch that was as pure a form of basketball as you're ever going to see."

Basketball is a team game, to be sure, one where success depends on five players being able to share one ball so that they bring out the best in each other. But there are times when an individual player gets so hot, his teammates know that the wisest course of action is to get out of the way, let him do his thing and just enjoy the show. When one player from each team gets hot like that, the show becomes a showdown that can be breathtaking to watch, particularly when the stakes are high.

Such was the case on May 22, 1988, when the Atlanta Hawks met the Boston Celtics in the deciding Game 7 of their Eastern Conference Semifinal playoff series. It was a pivotal game for the Hawks, who had made the playoffs nine times in 11 years but never gotten past the second round. The Celtics, meanwhile, had been to the NBA Finals four years in a row, winning a pair of titles, and were looking to make it back, so there was plenty at stake for them, too.

Each team featured a brilliant forward who would be named one of the NBA's 50 Greatest Players of All Time in conjunction with the league's silver anniversary celebration. The Celtics were led by Larry Bird, a great shooter and passer whose court sense and dedication to fundamentals and team play made him a throwback to players from an earlier era. The Hawks' star was Dominique Wilkins, whose aerial acrobatics earned him the nickname "the Human Highlight Film" and who was one of the most prolific scorers in NBA history.

Although they played the small forward position, Bird and Wilkins both were accomplished rebounders who were just as comfortable mixing it up in the paint as shooting from outside. Bird, 31, was an inch taller than the 6-foot-8 Wilkins, but the Atlanta star's superior jumping ability more than made up for the difference. Wilkins guarded Bird most of the time, but when Atlanta had the ball, the lanky 6-11 McHale usually had the assignment of trying to contain Wilkins.

While it was building all game long, the shootout really began in earnest in the fourth quarter, with the score tied 86-86 and 10:26 to play. With the season on the line, the two stars stepped to the forefront. "They each put their team on their back and said, 'Let's go,'" said Hawks coach Mike Fratello.

Bird fired the first salvo, a jumper with 10:03 to play, and went on to score nine points in 1:58. But Wilkins and the Hawks responded and refused to let the Celtics pull away, a basket by Wilkins tying the score again at 99-99 with 5:57 on the clock.

Bird scored 11 points after that, including a go-ahead basket with 3:34 left and a dazzling three-pointer over Wilkins at the 1:43 mark. "He hit that three-pointer with my hands dead in his face—what can you do?" Wilkins would say later.

What he could do was score 11 points of his own following Bird's go-ahead basket, including seven in the game's final 1:31, to keep his team in the chase.

"I thought I did everything I possibly could on the offensive end, and defensively I was all over him," said Wilkins. "He hit the big shots, I hit the big shots."

But in the end, Wilkins was put in a position where he had to miss. With Boston leading 118-115 and one second left, Wilkins was fouled and went to the line for two free throws. He made the first and then intentionally missed the second, in hopes that a teammate could get the rebound for a game-tying put-back. But Boston center Robert Parish batted the rebound to teammate Dennis Johnson and time expired, giving Boston the game and the series.

Wilkins came away dazzled by Bird's competitiveness. "Look in his eyes and you see a killer," he said of the Celtics star. Bird, meanwhile, said he came away from the game with more respect for the Hawks and Wilkins than he ever had before.

"I think I can safely say that, considering the stakes, the seventh game against Atlanta in 1988 was one of the greatest games ever played in the history of the league," said Bird. "That's a big statement, but I think I can back it up. We shot 60 percent from the floor and the Hawks shot 57 percent. There were only 15 turnovers between us. In the fourth quarter, each team scored on 17 of 22 possessions. And if you think all this means the defenses weren't very good, you couldn't be more wrong. The defense was aggressive both ways. It was just a high-level game from beginning to end."

Wilkins finished the game with 47 points, including 16 in the fourth quarter, having shot a stunning 19-for-23 from the field. "That's as hard as I've ever worked to guard a guy who wound up with 47," said McHale.

Bird, meanwhile, finished with 34 points on 15-for-24 shooting, getting 20 of his points in the final 10:03. "He wanted it," said Hawks assistant coach Don Chaney, who had been a teammate of Bird's late in his own playing career. "He wanted the ball and he came through. That's what superstars are made of."

"That's why I do all that shooting (in practice), in order to be able to have games like this," Bird said afterward. "You want to feel in control. There is no better feeling than to be in control of a basketball game and know your shot is going to open up every other aspect of your game, as well as help other players. I remember thinking during that fourth quarter that with the way Dominique was shooting, I had to make every shot. I came close, since I was 9-for-10!"

00:19

. . . .

Auerbach, Cousy, Russell
All Go Out Winners

Many contributed to the Boston Celtics' dynasty that accounted for 11 NBA championships in 13 seasons from 1957 through 1969, but three names stand out: Red Auerbach, Bill Russell and Bob Cousy. All three made their last seconds count, going out as champions.

Auerbach was the architect of those Boston teams and their coach through 1966, when he moved up to general manager. Russell was the only player to span those 13 seasons, the center whose defense and rebounding served as the team's backbone. He also was player-coach for the final three seasons, succeeding Auerbach on the bench. Cousy was the point guard and floor general whose time in Boston actually began before the dynasty but who went on to win six championships and set the standard of excellence for those who followed.

Each went out a winner, but none had it easy. The total margin of victory in the three Celtics' last games was a mere seven points.

Cousy came to the Celtics in 1950 after Boston first passed on the chance to draft him, then ended up with his rights, anyway, after losing a three-team lottery to determine to which teams the top players from the defunct Chicago Stags should go. "Little men are a dime a dozen. I'm supposed to win, not go after local yokels," said Auerbach, explaining why he picked 6-foot-11 Charlie Share over the 6-foot-1 Cousy, who played his college ball at nearby Holy Cross.

Cousy made Auerbach eat his words, leading the NBA in assists for eight consecutive seasons and quarterbacking the fast break that would become Boston's trademark. "The Houdini of the Hardwood," as he became known for his ballhandling prowess, was the prototype of the modern point guard, combining efficiency with his own special flair.

"Cooz was the absolute offensive master, the best point guard that ever played the game," said teammate Tom Heinsohn. "Once that ball reached his hands, the rest of us just took off, never bothering to look back. We didn't have to—he'd find us. Once you got in position to score, the ball would be there."

"The rest of us have to think about the things we do. He does them instinctively," said K.C. Jones, who succeeded Cousy as Boston's playmaker.

Cousy's last game as a Celtic came on April 24, 1963. Boston, leading the Lakers in the NBA Finals three games to two, was seeking to wrap up its fifth consecutive championship in Game 6 in Los Angeles and led by nine points early in the fourth quarter. But Cousy tripped, suffered a sprained left ankle and had to leave the game, and while he was on the bench, the Lakers closed the gap to one point. Cousy came back in at the five-minute mark to stabilize Boston's offense, and a steal and basket by Heinsohn put the Celtics up by four with two minutes to go. After that, Cousy's ballhandling baffled the Lakers, who were forced to foul in order to stop the clock. The Celtics hit their free throws, and finally Cousy dribbled out the final seconds of his career and tossed the ball high in the air as the buzzer sounded.

Auerbach, who joined the Celtics as coach in 1950-51 after three seasons with Washington and one with Tri-Cities, remained at the helm for 16 seasons and never once missed the playoffs. After leading Boston to its first title in 1957, Auerbach coached the team to a record eight in a row, beginning in 1959. His eighth and final championship as coach came in dramatic fashion.

The Celtics lost the opening game of the series to Los Angeles 133-129 in overtime, and just when all attention should have been focused on the Lakers, Auerbach made headlines by announcing that he would resign as coach following the series and turn the reins over to Bill Russell. That settled, the Celtics seemed to refocus on the series at hand and reeled off three wins in a row. The Lakers came back to win two and force a seventh game,

Boston's defense buckled down at the start of Game 7 and limited Lakers stars Elgin Baylor and Jerry West to a combined 3-for-18 from the field in the first half as the Celtics broke in front. But the Lakers rallied following intermission and whittled the lead down to six points with 20 seconds left. It still seemed safe for Auerbach to break out his trademark victory cigar, and he let Massachusetts governor John Volpe do the honors of lighting it for him. As the crowd surged toward the court, the Celtics turned the ball over and the Lakers scored; then it happened again. Suddenly, the lead was down to two points, with four seconds still on the clock. Some fans rushed onto the floor in a premature celebration, but this time the Celtics managed to hang onto the ball and K.C. Jones dribbled out the remaining time. After some moments of concern, Auerbach got to enjoy his final cigar.

The Celtics' string of championships came to an end in 1966-67, when they were beaten by the Philadelphia 76ers in five games in the Eastern Division Finals. The next year, however, they dethroned Philadelphia in seven games and then beat the Lakers in six for their first title with Russell as player-coach. In 1968-69, they did it again. Though they finished just fourth in the East with a 48-34 record, when it came playoff time, they were ready, beating Philadelphia in five and New York in six for another date against the Lakers in the finals.

This time the Lakers had the home-court advantage, which looked to be significant, as the home team won each of the first six games. Prior to Game 7, Lakers owner Jack Kent Cooke had thousands of balloons blown up and hung in the rafters at the Forum; he also had the Southern Cal marching band on hand, with orders to play "Happy Days Are Here Again" at the start of the anticipated postgame celebration. At least, that's the way the script read, a script that Auerbach, now the Celtics' general manager, got ahold of.

"Red mentioned that before the game," recalled Celtics forward Don Nelson, "and you could see the balloons by the thousands. It was definitely a mistake on their part to do that, and he just let his feelings be known."

The Celtics led by 17 in the fourth quarter, and Lakers center Wilt Chamberlain left the game with a bruised shin, but suddenly momentum began to shift. Los Angeles cut into the lead, but coach Butch van Breda Kolff refused to put Chamberlain back in. The Lakers' comeback fell short; Boston won 108-106, the clinching basket coming when Nelson grabbed onto a loose ball as the shot clock was running down and put up a foul-line jumper that hit the back rim, bounced straight up in the air above the top of the backboard, then plummeted through the net.

"That was the luckiest shot I ever made in my life," said Nelson. "Havlicek made a move, somebody from behind hit the ball and it came right to me. I was cutting across the paint. I just grabbed it and shot it very poorly, and it made that crazy bounce and went in. I just shot it too hard. I shot it very quickly and it hit the back of the rim and went up real high and came back through. There was no time to chuckle—it was like I planned it that way."

Russell, in his final game as player-coach, played all 48 minutes and hauled down 21 rebounds. Afterwards he announced his retirement, leaving with a remarkable statistic. In his NBA playoff career he played in 11 seventh games or deciding fifth games, and Russell's Boston Celtics won all 11.

00:18

. . . .

Indiana Gets Smart

When college basketball finally adopted the three-point field goal in 1986, rules guru Ed Steitz crossed paths with Indiana coach Bob Knight, one who is rarely quick to embrace change.

"He told me," Knight recalled, "'We put in the rule so you could win the national championship with Steve Alford.'"

But it was an old-fashioned two-point basket that would give the Hoosiers the crown, and it would be scored by a junior college transfer from Louisiana named Keith Smart rather than Alford, the homegrown hero who was the star of the Indiana team.

Knight had only begun accepting juco transfers into his program two years earlier, but Smart and Dean Garrett made him happy he did. Garrett, a 6-foot-10 center, gave the Hoosiers a shot-blocking presence and went on to a lengthy pro career, first in Europe and then in the NBA.

Smart's quickness and ability to penetrate and break down a defense was a perfect complement to Alford, a brilliant spot-up shooter and the only homegrown Hoosier on the team, a rare occurrence.

Whereas Alford was Indiana's "Mr. Basketball" in high school, Smart was yet to make his mark in the sport while growing up in Baton Rouge, Louisiana. He was only 5-foot-3 as a junior, and while he grew to 5-9 as a senior, a broken wrist ended any hopes of catching the eyes of college recruiters.

"I had the spirit," Smart said. "I just didn't have the body." He spent the next year working at a McDonald's to make money and working on his game in pickup action around town. He also grew to be six feet tall. Smart came to the attention of the coach at Garden City Community College in Kansas, who agreed to give him a tryout and liked what he saw. Smart played well for two seasons at Garden City, where his quickness piqued Knight's interest, and so Smart transferred to Indiana, where he averaged 11.2 points per game and shot .517 from the field and .841 from the foul line.

The team that made best use of the three-point field goal in 1986 was Providence. Coach Rick Pitino used a three-guard offense to get more shooters into the lineup, and instructed marksmen like Billy Donovan and Delray Brooks to spot up behind the three-point arc for their shots. Even on Friar fast breaks, if a layup wasn't available, the spot-up three-pointer was the shot of choice.

Providence upset Alabama and Georgetown to reach the Final Four, where it was beaten 77-63 by Syracuse when Donovan and Brooks could manage just one trey between them. Jim Boeheim's Orangemen disdained the three-pointer in favor of a power game built around center Rony Seikaly and forward Derrick Coleman, two future pros.

In the other bracket, Indiana used seven threes to erase a 14-point deficit and beat Auburn 107-90 in an early round, and a late bucket by Rick Calloway to cap a comeback from a 12-point second-half deficit and edge LSU 77-76 in the Midwest Regional final. The Hoosiers then went up against UNLV and outran the Runnin' Rebels 97-93 to move into the championship game. Interestingly, while UNLV was hoisting 35 three-pointers and hitting 13, Indiana was just 2-for-4 from behind the arc, taking care of business the old-fashioned way.

Syracuse tried several defenses against Indiana, including zones, man-to-man, and a box-and-one with 6-5 senior Howard Triche guarding the 6-2 Alford, a two-time All-American and Indiana's career scoring leader. Nonetheless, Alford shot 4-for-5 on threes including a pair in the last two minutes of the first half as Indiana took a 34-33 lead into intermission.

Alford, who finished with a game-high 23 points, hit another three treys in the second half before the box-and-one finally began to wear him down. He was scoreless in the game's final four minutes, his last basket of the game coming on a layup with 4:01 to play. But a team can't focus like that on one man without making itself vulnerable in other areas. "I've said all year long we're too good a team to have people just trying to contain me," said Alford.

The man who exploited that vulnerability was Smart, who scored 12 of his team's last 15 points and finished with 21 for the game. With Syracuse leading 61-56 and 7:22 to play, Smith—playing the championship game in his home state, in the Superdome in New Orleans—kept driving the ball to the basket and scored on three layups and one short shot within the lane.

Syracuse still led 72-70 with 38 seconds left when Triche made the first of two free throws but missed the second. Smart pushed the ball upcourt and scored on a short jumper, cutting the lead to one. After Syracuse got the ball inbounds, Smart immediately fouled Coleman, stopping the clock with 28 seconds to play. As Coleman, a freshman, went to the line for the one-and-one, Syracuse coach Boeheim elected not to put any players on the lane to contest a possible rebound, preferring to keep all his players back in an attempt to stop another transition basket.

Coleman missed the first (and only) free-throw attempt, Indiana got the uncontested rebound and Smart brought the ball over mid-court. He looked first to Alford, who was covered, then passed down low to Daryl Thomas. When Coleman and Triche collapsed on him, Thomas dished it back out to Smart, who was cutting toward the left baseline. He put up a 16-footer that went through with five seconds on the clock, stunning Syracuse and giving Knight his third NCAA title.

"We went inside to Thomas and Thomas made a great play getting the ball back out to Smart," said Knight. "I didn't know if his shot was going to go in or not, but hell, he got an open 16-foot shot from the baseline and he drilled it. I keep saying I didn't think this was a great team, but there was a great quality to this team, with its ability to play in crucial situations and its ability to make points."

While it was a two-pointer by Smart that proved decisive, the three-pointer did come into play in the championship game. Indiana made seven shots from behind the three-point arc, all by Alford, compared to four for Syracuse. "If not for the three-pointer, we'd be national champions," noted Boeheim.

Knight responded by telling the assembled media about his preseason conversation with Steitz. "Thanks, Ed," he concluded, with a smile.

00:17

• •

Princeton's Amazing Comeback

One of the more spirited rivalries in college basketball is between Penn and Princeton, perennial contenders for the Ivy League title. The reason is that more than a conference championship is at stake when these teams meet each other. While the champion receives an automatic berth in the NCAA Tournament, the loser is relegated (at best) to the NIT, since the Ivies usually are not considered a strong enough conference to rate two spots in the NCAA field. North Carolina can lose to Duke in the ACC Tournament, knowing it will get a berth in the NCAAs anyway. It doesn't work that way when Penn and Princeton meet, as they did on Tuesday, February 9, 1999, at the Palestra in Philadelphia, a game unlike any other between the two rivals.

Brian Earl of Princeton scored the first basket of the game, a three-pointer, but Princeton would not score again until 5:33 remained in the first half. By the time Chris Young stepped to the foul line to end the drought, Penn had reeled off 29 consecutive points and shell-shocked Princeton had been serenaded to several choruses of "You have three points!" from the Penn student section.

After Penn's 29-point run, Princeton went into halftime trailing 33-9, having shot 2-for-18 from the field. There was no pep talk from Princeton coach Bill Carmody; none was necessary. "It was obvious," said Earl. "We were getting killed. The offense was horrible. The defense was horrible. I was upset with myself and the team."

The teams traded baskets for nearly five minutes of the second half, and when guard Michael Jordan hit a three-pointer with 15:11 to play, Penn led by a seemingly comfortable 27 points. But Princeton reserve Mason Rocca answered with a three-pointer, Earl made a steal and another three, and suddenly there was a shift in momentum. "It was like an imperceptible riptide," said Princeton athletic director Gary Walters, a former Tiger hoopster. "You couldn't see it on the surface, but it was dragging them out and dragging us in."

Suddenly, all the Princeton shots that had been clanging off the rim were going in, all the passes that had been off target were finding their men. The defense, once porous, turned impenetrable, as senior Gabe Lewullis, playing on sore knees, made three steals and several other tips. What began as a push to make the final score respectable gradually changed into what seemed unthinkable during the first half—Princeton had a chance to win.

Princeton outscored Penn 23-2 over a stretch of nine minutes to close the gap to 45-39. Following two exchanges of baskets, Chris Young of Princeton hit an eight-footer, stole the ball and sank a three-pointer to make it 49-46. After a traveling call on Penn's Matt Langel turned the ball over, Earl faked a three-pointer and hit a driving layup and Princeton was within one.

Another turnover gave the ball back to Princeton, and Young, a freshman center, hit a hook shot for a 50-49 lead with 2:16 to play. It was the Tigers' first lead since the opening basket of the game.

There was still plenty of time left for Penn, but the Quakers could not cash in on three scoring chances. Forward Paul Romanczuk missed the front end of a one-and-one with 2:03 to play, and center Geoff Owens, who had just blocked a shot attempt by Young, missed two foul shots with 45 seconds left. Langel was called for a blocking foul with 17.7 seconds left, but Rocca missed the first of a one-and-one for Princeton, and the Quakers had one last opportunity.

Jordan looked to drive on Princeton defensive ace Ahmed El-Nokali, but when Earl came over to double-team, he kicked the ball over to Langel, who drove to his right and put up a 14-foot jumper that bounced off the rim. The rebound bounded toward the baseline, where Lewullis tipped it to Earl, who grabbed it as the final buzzer sounded.

"I've been doing games here since '55, and there's never been one like that. Never," said official scorer Bob McKee.

"I don't think there are any words for it," echoed Langel, who then was asked about the final shot. "I got the ball, I got a good look at it, it just didn't go down. It's supposed to go in and we run to the locker room winners. It didn't happen that way."

Penn coach Fran Dunphy was not about to blame the loss on Langel's miss. "It never should have come down to the last shot," he said. "We just succumbed to the pressure a little bit. It was a remarkable turn of events."

"You never think this could happen to you," said Jordan. "We blew it in the second half. We just choked."

Princeton's comeback to win from a 27-point deficit was the greatest in Ivy League history and the fourth-best in NCAA annals. The record is held by Duke, which trailed Tulane by 32 points with two minutes remaining in the first half but rallied to win 74-72 on Dec. 30, 1950. By another measure, Princeton's comeback comes out on top: The 27 points Princeton overcame represented 54 percent of its scoring in the game, while Duke's 32 points overcome represented 43 percent of its scoring.

No matter where it stands in the record books, it's a game that Earl, the leading scorer with 20 points, will never forget.

"At halftime we just said, 'Let's just try to save some face,'" he recalled. "Come out and show you can play on this floor, in front of the crowd. I don't know what happened or how it happened. We just kept playing and playing, then we were up one.

"It was just so frantic, the last couple of seconds. I don't know if I've ever felt better than that. To give everything you have is emotionally draining, and when I got that rebound and I heard that buzzer, I broke down. I had nothing left, both physically and mentally. I grabbed the ball and it all just sank in.

"I never expected to be in a game like this—completely opposite halves. It's funny. You always say when you're in a game like this, 'Hey, you know, they beat us by 20-something in the first half, but we can go back out there and beat them by 20-something in the second half.'

"I don't know how much you believe it. I don't know how much I believed it."

Believe it. Princeton, trailing 33-9 at the half and by 27 with 15:11 to play, beat Penn 50-49.

00:16

•••••••••••••••••••••••••••••

Charlotte Smith
Beats the Clock

Sometime it's in the genes.

As anyone who saw him will tell you, David Thompson was an amazing basketball player. Despite battles with drug abuse and injuries that kept him from achieving the true level of greatness that should have been his, once Thompson stepped in between the white lines of the basketball floor, there was nothing that was beyond his reach.

One of his nicknames was "Skywalker," and indeed he seemed able to defy gravity. Like a select few—Connie Hawkins, Julius Erving, Michael Jordan, Darnell Hillman and playground legend Herman "Helicopter" Knowings come to mind—the slender, 6-foot-4 Thompson would take off from around the foul line and glide toward the basket, and just when you'd expect him to start to come down, he'd rise to yet a higher plane and slam the ball through the net. He developed his jump shot, just as Erving and Jordan did as their careers wore on, but what you really paid your money to see was Thompson ahead of the field on a breakaway.

Thompson, who led North Carolina State to the 1974 NCAA title before averaging 22.1 points per game in a pro career that burned out after just nine seasons, was sitting with his niece, Charlotte Smith, who played for the North Carolina basketball team that was about to participate in the 1994 women's Final Four at the Richmond (Va.) Coliseum.

"Maybe two decades later, it will be your niece who wins a national title," Smith suggested to her uncle.

Two decades later, she did.

The 6-foot Smith set an NCAA Women's Final Four record by grabbing 23 rebounds as North Carolina edged Louisiana Tech 60-59 for the title. The 23 matched her uniform number, a number she chose not in honor of ex-Tar Heel Michael Jordan but for her mother, Etta, who wore that number in high school.

In addition to dominating the boards, Smith also sank the basket of her life as time was running down in what ranks as the most exciting women's championship game in NCAA history.

Pam Thomas had given Louisiana Tech a 59-57 lead with 14 seconds to play by sinking a jumper from 16 feet out. North Carolina worked the ball around to Tonya Simpson for a driving layup, but she missed the shot, and a scramble for the rebound resulted in a jump ball. North Carolina retained possession with four seconds to play, thanks to the alternating arrow. Sylvia Hatchell, the North Carolina coach, called a timeout to map a final play, then took another timeout. But when the Tar Heels put the ball in play, it was knocked loose and out of bounds before they could get a shot off.

Now there was just seven-tenths of a second left on the game clock—enough time for a Tar Heel to catch and shoot, but not much else. A two-pointer would tie the game and a three-pointer would win it, but with so little time, the goal was to get off the best shot possible from whatever distance. As junior forward Stephanie Lawrence looked to toss the ball in play, the Louisiana Tech defenders clogged the middle to prevent Smith or 6-foot-5 North Carolina center Sylvia Crawley from getting a close-in shot. North Carolina's other options appeared to be Sampson or point guard Marion Jones from outside.

Smith gave the Tar Heels another option. Once Lawrence was given the ball, Smith moved out from the lane to the right side and found an open area just beyond the three-point line. The Lady Techsters didn't follow her, since Smith, who regularly dunked in practice, was known for her inside game and not as a long-distance shooting threat. They preferred to stuff the lane and keep the ball from getting to Crawley.

With only seven-tenths of a second on the clock, Lawrence knew there was time only for the inbounds pass. Whoever caught it wouldn't have time to throw another pass or make her own move to the basket. She'd have to be open enough to get off her own shot right away. So when she saw Smith flash out to the right side, she knew this was the best opportunity for the Tar Heels.

Lawrence's pass was on target. Smith caught it and, without hesitating, rose up and launched her jumper from just beyond the three-point arc, the buzzer sounding soon after the ball left her right hand. Her form was perfect—a quick glance at the North Carolina jersey with the No. 23 on it conjured up the image of Jordan hitting the game-winner against Georgetown from the left side in the 1982 NCAAs.

Smith's shot found its mark, sailing cleanly through the net to give North Carolina, which had finished last in the Atlantic Coast Conference only three years earlier, its first-ever NCAA women's basketball championship. It also touched off a huge celebration as Smith was engulfed by her exuberant teammates.

"I just prayed and shot," she said afterward. "Then the mob hit me."

And 20 years after her uncle, David Thompson, had led N.C. State to the men's title, Smith had beaten the clock to give North Carolina the women's crown.

00:15

• •

Jordan's Jumper, Worthy's Steal Give Smith His First Title

It was a tough spot for a freshman, the closing seconds of the 1982 NCAA championship game between North Carolina and Georgetown, a one-point game that was very much up for grabs. But despite the presence of veterans like forward James Worthy and center Sam Perkins in his lineup, it was a slender 6-foot-6 freshman named Michael Jordan whom Dean Smith turned to when he drew up the Tar Heels' final play.

The game had been close throughout. Georgetown's 7-foot freshman center, Patrick Ewing, started things off by swatting away just about anything that approached the basket and North Carolina's first four baskets came on goaltending calls—it would be eight minutes before the Tar Heels would actually get the ball through the basket. That was what Georgetown coach John Thompson wanted. He was willing to endure some goaltending violations if the specter of the shot-blocking Ewing could be planted in the psyches of the top-ranked Tar Heels. "We wanted them to be conscious of Patrick," he said.

Georgetown led 32-31 at halftime, then the teams exchanged punches and counterpunches through a pulsating second 20 minutes in which the advantage swung back and forth and neither club ever led by more than four points. A short jumper in the lane by Eric "Sleepy" Floyd gave Georgetown a 62-61 lead with 57 seconds left to play. North Carolina ran 25 seconds off the clock, then called a timeout to set up a play.

Worthy, an All-American known for his slashes to the basket who had scored 28 points on 13-for-17 from the field, seemed the most likely candidate, because if he didn't hit his shot, he might well draw a foul. Instead, Smith decided to use Worthy as a decoy and have Jordan take the shot.

"I expected Georgetown to come back to the zone and jam it in," said Smith. "I said, '(Matt) Doherty, take a look for James or Sam, and Jimmy (Black), the crosscourt pass will be there to Michael.' As it turned out, Michael's whole side of the court was wide open because they were chasing James."

Black, North Carolina's point guard, faked a pass into the pivot, and when Georgetown defender Sleepy Floyd started to peel back for a double-team, Black swung the ball to a wide-open Jordan.

"I was all kinds of nervous," Jordan said. "But I didn't have time to think about doubts."

Jordan got the ball on the left side, not far from the baseline, and without hesitation, put up a 16-foot jumper. "I didn't look at the ball at all," said Jordan. "I just prayed. I had a feeling it was going in, but I didn't see it go in." It sailed through with 15 seconds remaining, pushing North Carolina in front 63-62.

"That shot put me on the basketball map," said Jordan.

"You hear a lot about Michael Jordan's shot. That certainly broke our backs, but we were having a lot of difficulty with Worthy," said Georgetown coach John Thompson. "Worthy was really hurting us, and at that point I thought they would get the ball in to James. Carolina sent Michael to the side opposite the ball, and we wanted to collapse back if James got the ball and not give him any room." Instead, the Tar Heels found Jordan on the weak side, and he nailed the jumper.

Now it was Georgetown's turn. Sophomore point guard Fred Brown brought the ball upcourt and sought to set up a shooter. He first looked to the left baseline for Floyd, like Worthy a consensus All-American, but the North Carolina defense was keying on him and had shut down the passing lane. Brown next turned to the middle of the floor, hoping to get the ball into the low post to Ewing or the Hoyas' other big man, Ed Spriggs. But there was a cluster of bodies in the lane and Brown didn't want to risk an entry pass.

With everyone else covered, Brown figured senior Eric Smith would be open on the right wing. "I thought I saw Smitty out of the right corner of my eye," Brown said. "My peripheral vision is pretty good, but this time it failed me. It was only a split second, but that's all it takes to lose a game."

The player Brown thought was Smith turned out to be Worthy, and Brown's pass went straight to the North Carolina forward. It went into the books as a steal, because there existed no other terminology for it; in tennis it would have been characterized as an unforced error. No one in the crowd of 61,612 at the Louisiana Superdome or among the millions watching on television was more shocked than Worthy himself.

"I thought he'd try to lob it over me or throw it away from me," Worthy said. "I was surprised that it was right in my chest."

"I think it was more of a reflex action, because Worthy had run out of the defense," said Thompson.

"James had gone for a steal on a fake moments earlier and was out of position," confirmed Smith. "He shouldn't have been where he was on the court, and it fooled Brown, and James went for the steal."

"I knew it was bad as soon as I let it go," Brown said. "I wanted to reach out and grab it back. If I'd had a rubber band, I would have yanked it back."

Worthy caught the pass with five seconds left and dribbled three seconds off the clock before Smith could catch him and foul him. He missed both free throws, but it didn't matter, as Georgetown only had time for a desperation heave by Floyd that was off target.

In his seventh trip to the Final Four, Dean Smith was finally going home a winner.

"This is one we'll always remember," said Worthy, who was chosen the Most Outstanding Player of the Final Four. "It was the one that made us and Dean Smith champions."

"I got my net," said Smith, holding up a string from one of the baskets that had been cut down during the celebration. "Sitting on the bench, it really was just another game, but now it's not."

As the North Carolina players celebrated the victory in the massive Superdome, Thompson, a 6-foot-10 bear of a man, wrapped a protective arm around Brown and tried to console the player whose turnover had ended Georgetown's chances. Asked what words were exchanged, Brown said, "He told me that I had won more games for him than I had lost. He said not to worry."

Brown then put the play in its proper perspective. "This is part of growing up," he said. "It was a great game. I loved playing it. I just wish the score was reversed at the end."

00:14

••••••••••••••••••••••••••••

N.C. State's Charles Dunks Phi Slamma Jamma

"The team with the most dunks wins the game. That's our slogan," declared Houston coach Guy Lewis, whose high-flying Cougars were the brothers of Phi Slamma Jamma, the fraternity of dunk.

So it was ironic that Houston should lose the 1983 NCAA championship game on a last-second dunk by North Carolina State's Lorenzo Charles.

N.C. State entered the title game with a record of 25-10, seeking to become the first team to win an NCAA championship with a double-digit loss total. In the final regular-season polls, the Wolfpack were ranked 16th by AP, 14th by UPI.

Houston, on the other hand, stood atop both polls with a 31-2 record and a lineup of tall, agile athletes who made NBA coaches drool with envy. The Cougars, who had been to the Final Four the previous season, were led by 7-foot center Hakeem Olajuwon and forward Clyde Drexler, two future all-pros. Their freshman point guard, Alvin Franklin, was the only starter under 6-foot-6, and players like Larry Micheaux, Michael Young, Benny Anders and Reid Gettys made them an exciting and formidable foe.

The Wolfpack had no intention of getting into a run-and-dunk contest with the Cougars.

"I've never seen anything like that in 16 years of coaching college basketball," North Carolina State coach Jim Valvano said after watching Houston's dunking exhibition in a 94-81 victory over Louisville in the national semifinals. "We'll try to handle their team by playing, shall I say, a slower tempo. If we get the opening tip, we may not take a shot until Tuesday morning."

Since the title game was being played on Monday night, Valvano was exaggerating, but not by much. N.C. State's lineup included 6-11 Thurl Bailey, who would enjoy a long and productive NBA career, but its strength was the veteran backcourt of Sidney Lowe (a future NBA player and coach) and Dereck Whittenberg, who were expert at controlling the tempo of a game. Also, despite their 10 losses, they were coming into the title game on a roll, having won their regional with a 63-62 victory over top-seeded Virginia before beating Georgia 82-77 in the semifinals.

"So many things have been happening right for us," said Bailey, "we might be catching them at the right time."

Even Valvano allowed for the possibility of an upset. "If the score is 100 to something, we're not going to win the game," he said. "But if it's in the 50s...."

Bailey scored the opening basket of the game on a dunk, then N.C. State focused on keeping the score down. The Wolfpack played a deliberate offense while using a zone defense that sagged around the basket to try to limit Houston's fast breaks. The strategy proved effective, as Houston managed just one dunk in the first half and had to settle for mostly jump shots. The result was a .313 shooting percentage for the half, which left the Cougars trailing 33-25 at halftime. What's more, Drexler picked up four personal fouls in the half.

Despite Drexler being on the bench, Houston broke loose after intermission and outscored N.C. State 17-2 to move in front

42-35 midway through the second half. That's when Lewis took Olajuwon out for a rest and pulled the reins on his team, ordering it into its "locomotion" offense, a slowdown style in which the players work the ball around in an attempt to generate layups.

Micheaux, for one, among the Houston players, didn't like the idea. "I felt that we should have kept playing the way we were playing," he said. "Our game is to get up and down the floor and dunk the ball."

Lewis' move backfired. The slowdown allowed N.C. State to catch its breath and regroup and took Houston out of its rhythm —the Cougars would get just four baskets the rest of the way. And Houston, with the exception of Drexler, was a poor free-throw shooting team, so Valvano ordered his players to foul at every opportunity. The Wolfpack gradually came back, closing to within two when Whittenberg hit a long jumper after Young missed the front end of a one-and-one, then finally drawing even on a 24-footer by Whittenberg that made it 52-52 with 1:59 to play.

At this point, Valvano told his players to try to foul Franklin, and sure enough, the freshman missed the front end of the one-and-one. N.C. State held onto the ball for the final shot and tried to set up Whittenberg, who had the hot hand, but Bailey's pass was tipped away by Drexler. Whittenberg managed to get to the ball anyway, but he was 30 feet from the basket and time was running out. He put up a desperation, off-balance shot, but it was short of the rim.

Charles, a 6-7 sophomore who spent much of the night going up against Olajuwon, saw exactly what was happening and slipped past the Houston center toward the basket.

"I knew when Whit let the shot go that it was short," Charles said. "I didn't know where Hakeem was, just that he was behind me. I knew I was the closest one to the basketball."

Charles caught Whittenberg's shot in the air just in front of the basket and dunked it with one second remaining, giving the

Wolfpack a 54-52 victory and the championship. TV cameras caught the emotional Valvano racing onto the court like a madman, looking for someone, anyone, to hug amidst the wild celebration.

"We figure the team with the most dunks will win," Olajuwon had said, echoing his coach's philosophy. And that's exactly what happened—Houston was beaten with its own favorite weapon. Charles' shot gave North Carolina State the edge in dunks, 2-1.

00:13

. . . .

Henderson's Steal Saves the Celtics

Of the three most famous steals in the storied history of the Boston Celtics franchise, two were by Hall of Famers—John Havlicek against Philadelphia in 1965 and Larry Bird against Detroit in 1987. But while he'll never make the Hall of Fame, Gerald Henderson got a steal that was the only one that came in the NBA Finals, when the Celtics were facing the Los Angeles Lakers in 1984.

It was a series fans had been awaiting ever since the Lakers' Magic Johnson, then playing for Michigan State, beat an Indiana State team led by Bird for the 1979 NCAA title in one of the landmark games in college basketball history. The teams had met twice each year during the regular season, and these were much-anticipated events that always were nationally televised and drew media from around the country. But this was the first time the two superstars—who were taking pro basketball to a new level of popularity— would meet for the NBA championship.

Johnson had led the Lakers to NBA titles in 1980 and 1982, while Bird had helped the Celtics to the crown in 1981. But Los Angeles' victories had been against Philadelphia, Boston's against Houston. Fans were eager to see what would happen when Johnson and Bird went head-to-head with the title on the line.

"It's like the opening of a great play. Everyone's waiting to see it," said Lakers general manager Jerry West.

The Lakers went into Boston and grabbed Game 1 115-109 behind 32 points by Kareem Abdul-Jabbar. Game 2 was a must-win situation for Boston, yet thanks to James Worthy's 29 points on 11-for-12 shooting, the Celtics found themselves trailing 115-113 with 18 seconds left. When Boston's Kevin McHale missed two free throws at that point, and Los Angeles got the rebound and Johnson called a timeout, it looked like the Lakers would be heading home with a formidable 2-0 series lead.

Johnson's timeout call, however, was just what Boston needed. Lakers coach Pat Riley had wanted the timeout only if McHale made his free throws. After the miss, he did not want a stoppage but preferred that his team run time off the clock and force Boston to foul. But Johnson misunderstood, and the timeout gave Boston a chance to get its players set up in a full-court press on defense. Still, all the Lakers needed to do was inbound the ball and maintain possession and the Celtics would be forced to foul.

Worthy passed the ball inbounds to Johnson, who returned it to Worthy deep in the right corner, near the Boston baseline. As McHale and Danny Ainge raced over to try to trap Worthy, the Lakers forward spotted teammate Byron Scott on the other side of the floor, seemingly open, and tossed a crosscourt pass in his direction.

But Henderson, who had briefly stepped away from Scott to protect against a pass downcourt, saw that Worthy was in danger and that Scott was his most likely outlet. He anticipated the play, stepped into the passing lane and picked off the ball. One dribble later, he sailed in for the game-tying layup with 15 seconds to play.

Henderson's game-saving steal so rattled the Lakers that Johnson let the final seconds of regulation play tick away without getting a shot off. The game went into overtime tied at 115-115, and Henderson set up Scott Wedman for the key basket in the five-minute extra period, helping the Celtics to a 124-121 victory.

Boston eventually won the series in seven games for its 15th NBA championship, and it was Henderson's steal that turned the tide.

"To be honest, if it wasn't for that steal, we probably would have been swept," said Bird.

Considering that the Lakers routed Boston 137-104 in Game 3 in Los Angeles, Bird's point is a valid one. Without Henderson's steal, the Celtics would have been in an 0-3 hole, a hole out of which no team has ever dug itself in the history of the NBA play-offs.

"What will I remember most from that series?" said Lakers coach Pat Riley. "Simple. Game 2. Worthy's pass to Scott. I could see the seams of the ball, like it was spinning in slow motion, but I couldn't do anything about it."

"I guess what I'll be remembered for in my career is that steal," said Henderson, a 6-foot-2 guard who went on to play 13 NBA seasons for eight teams. "People mention it to me all the time. But in that same game, in overtime, I like the play where I set up Scott Wedman for the winning jumper. That goes unnoticed, but I appreciate that play more than the steal. Those were the two points that won the game."

Nevertheless, the play that people remember is the game-saving steal. How does Henderson remember it? "We were pretty down after Kevin missed those free throws," he said. "M.L. (Carr) and I had been coming in as a defensive tandem for a while, and we'd tell each other, 'Let's make something happen. We've got to make it happen.' It wasn't hard to get pumped up with M.L. around.

"I had Byron Scott, and Magic took the ball out. He passed it to Worthy and I left my man, anticipating the play, because whoever went to double-team Worthy (in this case, Ainge) had left his man. I rotated to the open man. I guess it was an instinctive thing. I was at full speed. After I got it, Worthy came over. He wanted the ball back, but at that point, it's two."

Two points, Game 2 was tied and the Boston Celtics were saved.

00:12

· ·

When Villanova
Could Do No Wrong

Going into the 1985 NCAA championship game, all eyes were on Georgetown, the defending national champion that had lost only two games by a total of three points all season and was ranked No. 1 in the country. The Hoyas, who featured dominating center Patrick Ewing in the third Final Four of his career, had smothered St. John's 77-59 in the semifinals by playing a box-and-one defense, with David Wingate shadowing All-America Chris Mullin, who managed just eight points and had his streak of consecutive games scoring in double figures broken at 100.

"I'd have to put them with the great San Francisco teams of Bill Russell and the great Kentucky teams, Alex Groza and that club," St. John's coach Lou Carnesecca said of the Hoyas. "I'd also have to put them with the great UCLA clubs and the Indiana team (1976) that had five (future) pros. We tried everything, but when a club like Georgetown is performing at that level of proficiency, there's nothing you can do."

But one of the beauties, and one of the dangers, of the NCAA tournament is that it is a single-elimination event. An underdog can rise to the occasion, put it all together on the court for 40 minutes and defeat a team that, by all odds, it should have no business defeating.

Villanova was just such a team on April 1, 1985. The Wildcats had lost twice to Georgetown in the regular season and had dropped 10 games overall. None of the experts figured the Wildcats would beat Georgetown, but for 40 minutes they played near-perfect basketball and did just that.

Villanova shot a sizzling .786 from the field on 22-for-28, an NCAA-tournament record. In the second half they shot a mind-boggling 9-for-10 from the field; as the clock began winding down, they clinched the game from the foul line by sinking 11 free throws in the last 2:11. When it was all over, Villanova had a 66-64 victory and Georgetown coach John Thompson had his players applaud the victors in the postgame ceremony.

"Anytime you shoot that percentage," said Thompson, "you deserve the praise. You couldn't get much better."

Before the finals, that's what everyone was saying about Georgetown, including Villanova coach Rollie Massimino.

"Villanova is as good a team as has ever been assembled," said Massimino prior to the Final Four, "and that's only because of Patrick. He's the best to ever play college basketball. When it comes time to make the decision to win or lose in the last four minutes, he's involved in every single defensive play."

But when it came to playing defense, Villanova was no slouch. Its two regular season losses to Georgetown had come by scores of 57-50 and 52-50, the latter in overtime. And it had advanced to the title game by beating Memphis State 52-45, the fourth time in five tournament games it held an opponent under 50 points.

So while Massimino was lauding Georgetown and Ewing in public, in the privacy of his own team meetings he was conceding nothing. On the day of the final, he spoke to his players about the importance of a positive attitude. "I told all the kids to go to their rooms, sit for 15 minutes and tell themselves, 'You're not going to play to lose. You're going to play to win,'" said Massimino. "I told them, 'You can't play tentative; you can't play scared; you can't play not to lose. You're as good as the team you're playing tonight.'"

For that one night, they were even better.

As the first half wore on, the crowd that had expected Georgetown to dominate gradually began to sense the possibility of an upset and began rooting for the underdog, especially when the Wildcats held the ball for the final shot of the half and Harold Pressley made it for a 29-28 Villanova lead at intermission. The Wildcats, despite Georgetown's intense defensive pressure, shot 13-for-18 for the half.

Few expected Villanova to shoot as well in the second half; nobody expected the Wildcats to shoot better. Yet that's what they did in 20 minutes of brilliant basketball, as error-free a half as the tournament has seen. Offensively, they missed just one shot; defensively, they blanked Georgetown's Reggie Williams, who had 10 points in the first half, and held Ewing to six for a total of just 14.

And when the game was on the line and time was running down, they made the foul shots they had to make to win.

A 9-2 run early in the second half built a 38-32 lead for Villanova. But Georgetown, with Wingate picking up some of the scoring slack, roared back with a 10-3 run of its own to move in front 42-41. The Hoyas still led by one, at 54-53, when Villanova patiently worked the ball around for a good shot (the 45-second shot clock that had been used during the regular season was not being used in the NCAA tournament) and reserve guard Harold Jensen connected on a jumper from the right side for a 55-54 lead with 2:36 to play.

It would prove to be Villanova's last field goal of the game, but it was enough, as the Wildcats forced Georgetown into fouling situations and then cashed in their free throws. After Wingate was charged with an offensive foul, Villanova went into a delay game and the Hoyas had no choice but to foul. Ed Pinckney sank two free throws and Jensen netted four, and the Wildcats' lead was up to an insurmountable 61-56. Villanova went on to win 66-64.

The box score was something to behold. The 6-foot-9 Pinckney, named the Final Four's Most Outstanding Player, had 16 points, six rebounds and five assists and more than held his own against Ewing. Dwayne McClain led the Wildcats with 17 points, shooting 5-for-7 from the field and 7-for-8 from the foul line. Jensen hit all five field-goal attempts and was 4-for-5 from the foul line for 14 points off the bench. Point guard Gary McLain made all three field-goal tries, both foul-shot attempts and turned the ball over just twice in 40 minutes against Georgetown's vaunted pressure defense. The Hoyas shot 55 percent from the field, yet were outshot by more than 20 percentage points.

"It was frustrating," said Georgetown guard Harold Broadnax. "We were right in their faces (on defense) and they kept hitting and hitting."

Even the Wildcats recognized what an unusual performance they had turned in. "They're definitely the better team," Pinckney said of Georgetown. "If we played 10 times, they'd probably win a majority of them."

But in a one-game, winner-take-all situation, anything can happen. And on this night, everything went Villanova's way in 40 minutes of remarkable basketball.

00:11

. . . .

Loyola Stops Cincinnati's Run

Often in the heat of basketball battle, haste makes for waste. When the clock is running down, it's tempting for a player to rush his shot, trying to make sure he gets it off in time.

Vic Rouse resisted that temptation in the closing seconds of overtime in the 1963 NCAA championship game.

Rouse grabbed the rebound of a missed shot by Loyola of Chicago teammate Les Hunter and scored on a put-back with one second left in the extra period, giving the Ramblers a 60-59 victory over two-time defending champion Cincinnati. Loyola thus went home with an NCAA crown in its first appearance in the national tournament.

"I didn't tip it," Rouse said. "I grabbed it tight, jumped up and laid it in. I'd missed a couple like that before and I wanted to be so sure. Oh, my, it felt good!"

The title game had been projected as a battle of offense vs. defense, the unstoppable force meeting the immovable object. Loyola was the highest-scoring team in the country, averaging nearly 92 points per game. Cincinnati was the stingiest team in the land, allowing a mere 52.9 points per game. The prevailing wisdom was that the only way the Ramblers could win would be in a run-and-gun shootout, and that a tight, low-scoring game favored the more experienced and battle-tested Bearcats, the top-ranked team in the country.

Cincinnati succeeded in controlling the tempo, and still lost.

"Our game plan worked for us 99 out of 100 times," said Cincinnati guard Tony Yates. "On this night, it didn't."

Loyola won despite shooting 23-for-84 from the field, a meager .274 mark. But the Ramblers took care of the ball, committing only three turnovers in the overtime contest to 16 by Cincinnati. And despite falling behind early and trailing by as many as 15 points in the second half, when the opportunity to win presented itself, they didn't let it slip away.

The Ramblers got off to a miserable start, missing 13 of their first 14 shots. At halftime they were behind 29-21 and their leading scorer, Jerry Harkness, was without a field goal. Harkness admitted his confidence was shaken. "I didn't want to be embarrassed. I was thinking, 'Don't let them kill us.'"

It got worse in the first six minutes of the second half, as Cincinnati extended its lead to 45-30 and appeared well on its way to a third consecutive national title. Suddenly, with Loyola in a desperate full-court press and Cincinnati focusing more on trying to take time off the clock than trying to score, the Bearcats began to unravel. They started turning the ball over, missing whatever shots they did take, even missing from the free-throw line. Cincinnati center George Wilson picked up his fourth personal foul and had to sit out for four minutes. Yates and Tom Thacker also picked up their fourth fouls for Cincinnati, though they didn't come out. Nobody came out for Loyola—all five of the Chicago team's starters would go the entire distance.

Harkness finally scored his first basket with 4:41 to play, then he came up with a steal and scored again to cap a 15-3 run that brought Loyola back into contention at 48-45 with 4:26 remaining. Hunter cut the deficit to one, at 53-52, by tipping in a shot by Harkness, who quickly fouled Cincinnati's Larry Shingleton to stop the clock with 12 seconds to play. With a chance to put the Bearcats comfortably in front—remember, there was no three-point shot in 1963—Shingleton made the first free throw but missed the second.

Hunter grabbed the rebound and fired an outlet pass to Ron Miller, who seemed to run with the ball but managed to avoid a violation before passing off to Harkness. The 6-2 New Yorker, who didn't play organized basketball until his senior year of high school, recalls what happened next.

"I don't think I felt anything," he said. "When I shot, I normally had a touch for it. But this time I never felt it. It was almost like somebody guided it for me."

Harkness's shot was on target, tying the score at 54-54 with four seconds left, and time ran out before Cincinnati could stop the clock or get off a last-ditch attempt.

The teams exchanged baskets in overtime until it was 58-58, then Loyola tried to hold the ball for the last shot. But guard John Egan was tied up by Shingleton with 1:21 left, forcing a jump ball between the two smallest men on the court, both 5-foot-10.

Egan controlled the tip and Loyola again tried to hold for the final shot, preferably by Harkness. Although he was closely guarded by Cincinnati's Ron Bonham, Harkness realized time was running out and went up for his shot anyway. Bonham got a hand on the ball as Harkness was on his way up.

"I felt I was losing it," said Harkness. "I grabbed it again, then I saw Les out of the corner of my eye."

Instead of shooting, Harkness passed the ball to Hunter to the left of the lane. Hunter's shot hit the rim and bounced long, but Rouse, alone on the right side of the basket, collected the rebound and made sure of his put-back.

"I felt suspended in air—you could almost say it was an out-of-body experience—and totally focused," Rouse said of his game-winning offensive rebound. "It was like a blessing."

00:10

Cheryl Swoopes to the Hoop

One of the most exciting players in women's basketball history, Cheryl Swoopes has an exquisite sense of timing.

In college, she used the national platform of the 1993 NCAA championship game for one of her greatest performances, scoring a record 47 points as Texas Tech edged Ohio State 84-82 for the national title.

As a pro, she missed most of the inaugural season of the WNBA because she was pregnant with her first son, but after he was born, she came back in time to help the Houston Comets win the first league championship. Then she played a key role as the Comets successfully defended their title in 1998.

A 6-foot forward who could score from three-point range or slash to the basket, Swoopes was named National College Player of the Year at Texas Tech in 1993, only two years after she was honored as National Junior College Player of the Year in 1991 at South Plains (Texas) J.C. She ranked second in the nation in scoring at 28.1 points per game in 1992-93, then set 11 NCAA Tournament, Final Four or Championship records in a brilliant postseason.

Although she certainly saved her best for last, the rest of Swoopes' tournament wasn't exactly chopped liver. She poured in

36 points, nailing 15 of 16 free throws, as the Lady Raiders advanced to the Final Four with a 79-54 rout of Colorado. Earlier, despite a bruised knee suffered in the opening minute of play, she tallied 30 points in a 70-64 second-round win over Washington before a school-record crowd of 8,541 in Lubbock, and she scored 33 points in an 87-67 win over Southern Cal that marked Texas Tech's first NCAA victory away from home.

Prior to the Final Four in Atlanta, Swoopes was named the Division I Player of the Year and the Naismith Award winner as the top player in the nation. If those honors represented any extra pressure, she showed no ill effects, as she tallied 31 points as Texas Tech upset top-ranked Vanderbilt 60-46. Vanderbilt was within three with 4:52 left, but Swoopes hit a pair of baskets to enable Texas Tech to pull away.

That was only the appetizer. The main course came on April 4, when Swoopes set an NCAA championship-game record by scoring 47 points as Texas Tech won its first title.

Ohio State led 55-54 before Swoopes scored 16 of her points in the final 10 minutes and Texas Tech actually won more easily than the final score of 84-82 would indicate. A pair of baskets and a three-point play by Swoopes put Texas Tech in front 80-73 with 58 seconds left, and four free throws down the stretch nailed down the victory. Ohio State scored nine points in the final 31.8 seconds, including a pair of uncontested three-point shots, to make the score close.

The next day, a crowd of 40,000 welcomed the Lady Raiders back at a celebration in Lubbock's Jones Stadium. "We told you we'd go to Atlanta and do our best, and I guess we did," said Swoopes, who scored 54 percent of her team's points in the two Final Four games. "We kicked butt and took names and brought the national championship back to you guys!"

A little over a week later, Swoopes was drafted by the Daytona Beach team of the U.S. Basketball League, a men's pro circuit. "We watched her play," said one team official. "If we've ever seen a woman who had a shot of making a men's team and playing, she's it."

Swoopes, who led Texas Tech to a 58-8 record in her two All-American seasons, instead took her game to the women's professional league in Italy, where she averaged 23 points per game for Bari. She returned to play for the United States in the 1994 World Championships and the 1994 Goodwill Games, then joined the USA Basketball Women's National Team that practiced together and compiled a 52-0 record in the year leading up to the 1996 Olympics. At Atlanta, she averaged 13.0 points, 3.5 rebounds and 3.9 assists and shot .606 from the field in leading the United States to the gold medal, one that held special meaning for Swoopes. In 1992, as one of the youngest participants in the Olympic Trials and with no international experience, she was cut from the squad, one of the few times she has known anything less than success at basketball.

"I was just a baby at it. I was very young, and honestly, I had never really played against so many great, talented players," she said. But instead of giving up, she went to work on improving her game. "There's always something every day you can get better at, things you can work on. Of course, you get tired, and it's really hard to get out there and keep going all the time. But you have to remember, in the back of my mind, all I'm thinking of is '96, gold medal.... I just made myself come out every day and pushed myself."

The birth of the WNBA was important to Swoopes, one of the league's early marquee signings, but the birth of her son Jordan (yes, named after Michael Jordan, against whom Swoopes once played one-on-one; like Jordan, Swoopes has a Nike shoe named after her, the first woman with that distinction) was of greater importance. She joined the Houston Comets two weeks after Jordan was born and played a supporting role, appearing in nine games, as the Comets, led by Cynthia Cooper, won the league's first championship.

In 1998, she was named to the All-WNBA First Team after averaging 15.6 points, 5.1 rebounds and 2.48 steals per game. She ranked among the league leaders in all three categories, as well as three-pointers, three-point accuracy and free-throw accuracy. She had four double-doubles during the season as the Comets repeated as WNBA champions.

On July 27, 1999, Swoopes became the first woman in WNBA history to post a triple-double when she had 14 points, 15 rebounds and 10 assists for the Houston Comets in an 85-46 rout of the Detroit Shock.

00:09

• •

T-Spoon's Miracle Slows Comets, Can't Stop Their Three-Peat

Not even the most dramatic basket in the first three years of the Women's National Basketball Association could stop the Houston Comets from their three-peat.

With streamers and confetti already falling from the rafters of the Compaq Center in Houston in a celebration that would prove about 24 hours premature, Teresa Weatherspoon shocked and silenced the capacity crowd of 16,285—all of whom seemed to be dressed in red, the Comets' color—by sinking a 55-foot prayer to give the New York Liberty a 68-67 victory. That evened the best-of-3 1999 WNBA Finals at one victory apiece and prevented the Comets from celebrating a third consecutive league title in front of their home fans.

But only for a day. Even miracles don't last forever.

The Comets, who had beaten New York and Phoenix to win the first two WNBA crowns, bounced back from their stunning last-second defeat and stifled the Liberty with a tenacious defensive effort en route to a 59-47 victory on September 5, 1999. That completed Houston's charge to a third consecutive WNBA championship, a run the Comets dedicated to the memory of former teammate Kim Perrot, who died of cancer less than three weeks earlier.

"Kim's inspiration has been tremendous," said Comets coach Van Chancellor amidst the post-game celebration. "After all that this team has gone through, I don't know of any players at any time who have deserved something more. It doesn't get any better than this after yesterday."

"Yesterday" was a finish to the second game of the championship series that can only be described as unbelievable.

The Rockets had won the series opener at New York's Madison Square Garden 73-60, and everything was in place for a Texas-sized celebration when the teams met for Game 2 on Saturday, September 4. The trophy was in town, the champagne was on ice, the streamers and confetti were up in the rafters, all waiting for the right moment.

The Comets cooperated by jumping out to a big early lead, going up 37-19 with 1:44 left in the first half. But New York rallied and outscored Houston 24-3, pulling in front 42-40 on a three-pointer by Crystal Robinson with 11:55 to play.

"We didn't come out with intensity. We came out like we were going to cruise in the second half and they outplayed us," said

Houston star Cynthia Cooper. "We allowed them to come back and get into the game," echoed teammate Sheryl Swoopes. "Any time a team comes back from so far down, they steal the momentum."

Even though the Comets regrouped and reeled off eight points in a row to climb back on top, they could not put the Liberty away. New York scratched and clawed its way back again, finally edging in front 63-62 on five consecutive points by Kym Hampton. Two free throws by Swoopes and one by Thompson made it 65-63 in favor of Houston, but Robinson's jumper tied the score in the final minute.

That's when the Comets worked the ball to Thompson, who drove into the lane, spun toward the right baseline and put up an eight-footer that banked through to give the Comets a 67-65 lead with 2.4 seconds to play. Paper began to fall from the upper reaches of the Compaq Center and security guards ringed the court for the anticipated presentation of the championship trophy as the red-clad fans roared their approval.

New York was out of timeouts, so even though the clock stopped with Thompson's basket, the Liberty didn't have a chance to inbound the ball from midcourt, or even talk strategy with coach Richie Adubato. Rookie Becky Hammon hastily collected the ball out of bounds and tossed it in to Weatherspoon on the right side in the backcourt, some 75 feet from the Liberty basket.

T-Spoon took two dribbles, as many as she dared, and let fly with a shot from beyond the midcourt line. It arched toward the basket, kissed the top of the white box on the backboard behind the rim and then nestled through the net.

A three-pointer. Liberty wins, 68-67.

The crowd was stunned. On the court, where the trophy was about to have been presented, the Houston players stood in shock as members of the Liberty piled upon Weatherspoon in celebration.

"Nothing compares to this, nothing I have ever done," said Weatherspoon, who goes by the nicknames of Spoon and T-Spoon, the latter to differentiate her from teammate Sophia Witherspoon. "This is the biggest shot I've ever hit, the most excitement I've ever been involved with. I've made one of those before, but never in a game like this."

Actually, her other midcourt buzzer-beater wasn't too shabby. When she was a freshman at Louisiana Tech, she connected from the center stripe to beat top-ranked Southern Cal, a team that featured future Hall of Famer Cheryl Miller. But according to Spoon, that game-winner didn't compare to this one.

"Nope, no way. Not even in the same class," she said. "That wasn't for a shot at a championship."

While the Liberty didn't have a timeout in order to set up the final play, it was, in a sense, scripted. Several of the New York players, including Weatherspoon, liked to end their practice sessions by tossing up half-court bombs. Weatherspoon said she wasn't the best on the team in those games, but she got it right when it counted.

"I've watched Becky (Hammon) shoot those shots every day in practice," she said. "I just flipped it up there like she does and God pushed it in."

"They practice that shot every day after practice," confirmed Adubato. "It finally won a game for us. I always want to tell them to go in and shower, but they insist on shooting them for awhile. Now I am not going to tell them to shower."

"That was a great shot by Teresa Weatherspoon," said Chancellor, the Comets' coach. "This is the most heartbreaking loss I've been through."

On the court, that is. The biggest loss for the Comets in 1999 was the death of Perrot, the 5-5 point guard who had won on a spot on Houston's developmental roster in 1997 after an open tryout and eventually became the team's starting point guard. Perrot, who led the Comets in assists and steals in 1998, learned in February, 1999 that she was suffering lung cancer that had spread to her brain and was causing tumors. She made it to the Compaq Center for the

1998 championship banner-hanging ceremony on June 22, but died on August 19.

The Comets dedicated their quest for a three-peat to Perrot, and not even Weatherspoon's miraculous shot could stop them. Cooper, Perrot's best friend on the team who had missed the first game of her professional career on the night Perrot died, made certain of it.

Cooper scored 24 points in the deciding Game 3 to wrap up her third consecutive WNBA Finals MVP award as the Comets shook off the effects of their last-second loss and dominated New York. The Liberty shot just 31 percent from the field, was outrebounded 36-28 and was forced into 16 turnovers. No Liberty player scored over 11 points.

"After yesterday, today's game is the sweetest that it has ever been, I'll tell you that right now," said Chancellor.

"I love my teammates, I love them so much," said Thompson, who would have been the heroine of Game 2 had Weatherspoon's prayer not been answered. "We have so much heart, so much character. We never quit or gave up and we battled through so much. This season has been a struggle, we battled through what has been a very difficult stretch for us. We earned this championship the hard way, but it makes it that much sweeter."

"We really wanted to win it for Kim," said Cooper in accepting the Finals MVP trophy. "This is in memory of Kim; this is in tribute to Kim."

00:08

. . . .

Yes, UConn!

As the 1999 NCAA basketball tournament began, Duke looked to be in a class of its own.

With Elton Brand, college basketball's Player of the Year, and three teammates who would join him in being selected in the first half of the first round of the NBA Draft, the Blue Devils were loaded with talent. They had cruised through the regular season with just one loss, an early-season stumble against Cincinnati, knowing it was all just a preliminary to the NCAA Tournament, when they would be trying to establish their place in history. Duke, coached by Mike Krzyzewski, was tied with Kentucky at two championships and four Final Four appearances in the 1980s, and a victory in 1999 would establish the Blue Devils as college basketball's top team of the decade.

Most of the experts rated Connecticut as a solid second choice —probably better than anybody else in the country, but not quite up to Duke's level. What they couldn't accurately rate was Connecticut's desire.

In a state that had rallied round the school, especially when the UConn women went undefeated and captured the national title in 1995, Jim Calhoun's team was anxious to prove it was not No. 2 but No. 1, and that it could do better than its three Elite Eight appearances in the '90s. The Huskies also were playing for pride in a state that was sorely in need of an athletic lift after losing its only two pro franchises, the NHL's Hartford Whalers (to Carolina) and the ABL's New England Blizzard (to the league folding), and failing in a bid to lure a third, the NFL's New England Patriots.

When Duke could only beat Michigan State by a 68-62 count in a sloppy semifinal, there seemed to be a ray of hope for the Huskies, who in addition to all of the above, had revenge as a motivating force. In 1990, Connecticut had lost to Duke in the East Regional at the Meadowlands when the Blue Devils' Christian Laettner nailed a buzzer-beater for a 79-78 overtime victory.

It would take nearly a decade, but the Huskies would exact their revenge.

Calhoun and his staff approached the matchup with confidence. Whereas most teams were afraid to run against the athletic Blue Devils, Connecticut went into the game looking to run at every opportunity and force Duke to worry about explosive forward Richard Hamilton (himself a future NBA lottery pick) and rugged guards Khalid El-Amin and Ricky Moore. "The more tape we watched," said UConn assistant coach Tom Moore, "the more we learned that we're pretty quick ourselves." At the other end, the Huskies used a forward, usually Kevin Freeman, to join center Jake Voskuhl in double-teaming Brand, who would finish with 15 points and 13 rebounds but never took the game over, as he is so capable of doing. "I never knew where the double-team was coming from," he said later.

Duke jumped in front 9-2 but Connecticut refused to be rattled, going on a 15-4 run of its own that let Duke and the crowd of more than 40,000 at Field House in St. Petersburg know this would be no runaway. Duke led 39-37 at the half and 46-41 shortly after intermission, but again the Huskies responded, turning a five-point deficit into a four-point lead at 57-53. It would be close the rest of the way.

With 4:07 left, a timeout was called with the score tied at 68-68. "Me and Richard (Hamilton) looked at each other and said, 'It's winning time,'" said El-Amin.

A pair of free throws and a three-pointer by Hamilton, the game's leading scorer with 27 points, gave UConn a five-point lead, but one free throw by Chris Carrawell and a three-pointer by Trajan Langdon, Duke's top scorer with 25 points, closed it to one. El-Amin hit a floater over Brand with the shot clock winding down, but William Avery countered with two free throws to keep it at one, and after a missed shot by El-Amin, Duke had the ball with 20 seconds to go.

"I heard Coach K yelling to Trajan, 'Go get the ball and take him,'" said Moore. "I loved that. Him against me. All I had to do was get one stop. I started smiling because I knew he wasn't going to score that basketball. I knew it was him against me, and I knew my will to win would prevail."

Langdon faked and faked, trying to find a lane to drive to the basket or create enough space for a jumper. But whichever way Langdon turned, the tenacious Moore was in his path, finally forcing a traveling violation with 5.4 seconds left on the clock.

"I might have traveled, I might not have. That's the call," said Langdon. "But that's not the game. There's millions of plays in that game that determine the outcome, so I'm not going to hang my head on that play."

Duke fouled El-Amin on the ensuing inbounds play, and the Connecticut point guard made both for a 77-74 lead with 5.2 seconds to play—still enough time for Duke to get the ball into position for a three-pointer. Rather than call a timeout to set up a play, Langdon took the inbounds pass and raced upcourt, trying to get free for a shot. But before he could do so, he lost his balance and the ball skittered away, and the Blue Devils' hopes went with it.

Krzyzewski wouldn't second-guess the decision not to call a timeout with 5.2 seconds left. "Absolutely. Positively. Absolutely I want Trajan Langdon to take that shot," he said. "The ball was in our best player's hands with an opportunity to win the game."

"There were three people there," said Langdon of the final play. "I got tripped a little bit, but I tried to get the shot off and I was stripped."

"It was clean," said Krzyzewski. "Everything about the game was clean. You have to give them an immense amount of credit for making big plays in the second half, especially in the final eight minutes. Because we came back and made big plays, too."

After being denied a trip to the Final Four in three previous regional finals, the Huskies this time were going back to Storrs with the big prize. And they'd done it the hard way, beating the top-ranked team in the country, a team that was favored in the championship game by 9 points.

"The kids wanted Duke," said Calhoun. "They wanted to play the best and beat the best—and they did."

00:07

The One and Only Dream Team

What was the best basketball team of all time?

It was only together for seven weeks in the summer of 1992, but you'd be hard-pressed to find a better basketball team than the one that won the gold medal for the United States at the Summer Olympics in Barcelona—the original Dream Team.

There have been other Dream Teams since then; you can't stop the marketing machine of the NBA once it latches onto a good thing. But for basketball people, for anyone who appreciates the sport at its best, there was one, and only one, Dream Team.

"Dream Team is a lot of name to live up to," said Chuck Daly, the Hall of Famer who led the Detroit Pistons to a pair of NBA championships and was head coach of the Olympic team. "But if anything, the 1992 U.S. Olympic men's basketball team exceeded all hopes and expectations. I think we truly gave the world a glimpse —only a glimpse, since we were never seriously challenged—of what basketball can be like at its highest level."

This was the first U.S. Olympic team that was open to NBA players after the International Basketball Federation lifted a long-standing ban, and it got the cream of the crop. Each of the 11 NBA players chosen for the Dream Team (one college player also was selected) was an NBA All-Star many times over and a likely candidate for the Basketball Hall of Fame, many destined for election in the first year of eligibility.

Start with Michael Jordan, considered by many the greatest basketball player of all time and without question the most popular athlete of any team sport from a global perspective. Then there were the two elder statesmen and unofficial team captains, Magic Johnson and Larry Bird, who led their teams to eight NBA championships in the 1980s, won millions of new fans for the sport of basketball with their brilliant team-oriented style of play and forged one of the greatest rivalries in the history of team sports.

Sharing the point guard duties with Johnson was John Stockton, the NBA's career leader in assists and steals. For the shooting guard and small forward positions, in addition to Jordan and Bird, Daly had at his disposal Scottie Pippen, the offensive and defensive standout who teamed with Jordan to lead the Chicago Bulls to six NBA titles; Chris Mullin, one of the great pure shooters of all time and a certified gym rat with an unparalleled work ethic; and Clyde

Drexler, who was part of Phi Slamma Jamma at the University of Houston and then a mainstay of the Portland Trail Blazers before winning an NBA championship with the Houston Rockets.

Big men? Karl Malone, at 6-9 and 260 pounds, the prototype of the modern power forward, combining strength and speed, agility and aggressiveness, shared the position with the dynamic Charles Barkley, who compensated for his relative lack of height at 6-6 with remarkable strength and quickness. At center were two of the greatest all-around pivotmen of the modern basketball era: David Robinson, the Admiral with the outstanding all-around game, and Patrick Ewing, the "Hoya Destroya," whose defense anchored the great Georgetown teams of the early 1980s and who went on to become the all-time leading scorer and rebounder in New York Knicks history. Providing depth at both power positions was the lone representative from the college ranks, Christian Laettner, who led Duke to consecutive NCAA titles in 1991 and 1992, the leading scorer in the history of the NCAA tournament and the first man to start in four Final Fours.

Clearly, from 1 to 12 on the roster, this was the greatest assembly of basketball talent ever. But could they play together as a team? Would there be a clash of wills, or egos, among these players, each a front-line star in his own right? "The challenge is going to be our own people," said Daly. "How do we bring this team together in spirit and in thinking, as well as from a technical basketball standpoint?"

The tactful Daly was careful to parcel out playing time as evenly as possible. He actually was helped in this regard by a leg injury to Stockton that left him available only for spot duty in four games. The remaining 10 players shared the 200 available minutes per game (40 minutes at each of five positions) almost equally, with the collegian, Laettner, seeing only limited action.

The NBA and USA Basketball, the governing body for the sport in the United States, did everything to make the Olympic experience an enjoyable one for the players. Families were invited to be with the players throughout, from the training camp at a resort in La Jolla, California, to a pre-Olympic camp in posh Monte Carlo and then on to Barcelona, where they stayed in an air-conditioned hotel downtown and enjoyed tours of the city's attractions as well as tickets to various Olympic events. Wherever they went, the players and their families were treated like royalty, both figuratively and literally at a reception in Monaco hosted by Prince Rainier and Prince Albert.

The reaction to the Dream Team was remarkable. For many European fans, this was their first chance to see these stars of the NBA in person, and they took advantage of it. The games, of course, were sellouts, and hundreds of fans stood outside the team's hotel at all hours, day and night, just to catch a glimpse of the players as they went in and out. When Barkley decided he wanted to sample the tastes of Las Ramblas, Barcelona's main drag, he became a pied piper, leading fans of all ages from one stop on the street to another.

"It was like Elvis and the Beatles put together," said Daly. "Traveling with the Dream Team was like traveling with 12 rock stars, that's all I can compare it to. Everywhere we went, from San Diego to Portland to Monte Carlo to Barcelona, people couldn't get enough of us."

The fact that the Dream Team was head and shoulders above the level of its opposition seemed to bother only critics in the United States who were looking for nits to pick. Other teams loved competing against these living legends, whether in the pre-Olympic qualifying tournament in Portland or in the Olympics itself. One player from Puerto Rico was guarding Magic Johnson during the qualifying tournament, and when he should have been concentrating on his man, instead he was frantically waving to a teammate on the bench with a camera to take a picture of them together. In fact, a new pregame ritual developed where the opposing team would gather around the Americans for a two-team photograph before each game.

The photo-taking continued at the Olympics. "When I was playing," said Arturas Karnisovas of Lithuania, who played college ball in the United States at Seton Hall, "I told our manager to take a few pictures of me guarding Barkley. Then, when I was on the bench, I decided to take a few more shots. These are the stars from the stars."

Marcelo Milanesio, Argentina's point guard, summed up the feelings of opponents: "Without any doubt, not just for us but for everyone playing in this tournament, it is great to play with Michael Jordan and Magic Johnson. I am so overwhelmed with joy."

"They knew they were playing the best in the world," said Daly. "They'll go home and for the rest of their lives be able to tell their kids, 'I played against Michael Jordan and Magic Johnson and Larry Bird.' And the more they play against our best players, the more confident they're going to get."

Indeed, the latter was one reason the ban on NBA players was lifted. To promote the global growth of the sport, International Basketball Federation head Boris Stankovic felt it was vital for teams from around the world to see, and compete against, the very best. "We needed to get things moving and make basketball the No. 1 game in the world," said Stankovic. "I thought the only way to do that was to involve NBA stars. My hope was that when everyone saw how good they were, it would force other countries to catch up with the United States."

The Dream Team went through the Olympics virtually untested, winning its opener against Angola 116-48 and its eight games by an average of nearly 44 points. If there was a nervous moment, it came in the gold medal game, when the team from Croatia that included Toni Kukoc, Dino Radja and Drazen Petrovic led 25-23 midway through the first half. But Barkley hit a three-pointer and set up Drexler for a basket, the U.S. led by 14 at halftime and coasted to a 117-85 victory.

Barkley was the team's leading scorer, averaging 18 points per game, with Jordan (14.9), Malone (13.0), Mullin (12.9) and Drexler (10.5) also averaging in double figures and Robinson, Ewing, Bird, Pippen and Johnson each at 8 ppg or more. Ewing and Malone shared rebounding honors at 5.3 rebounds per game, and Pippen, assuming more of the playmaking responsibilities in light of injuries to Stockton and Johnson, led the way with 5.9 assists per game.

There was some competition, however. On July 22 in Monte Carlo, a week before the start of the Olympics, the Dream Team engaged in a closed, intra-squad scrimmage witnessed only by a few officials from USA Basketball and others in the traveling party. Played with referees and a 20-minute clock to simulate game conditions, it may well be the greatest basketball game the public has never seen.

On one side were Johnson, Bird, Ewing, Barkley and Mullin; on the other, Jordan, Pippen, Robinson, Malone and Laettner (Stockton and Drexler sat it out due to injury). "It was as good a demonstration of basketball as I've ever seen in my life, everything a basketball player could want," said Johnson. It also led to some serious trash-talking, which provided insight into the competitive fire of these great athletes, and especially Jordan.

"We were leading 14-2 and I let Michael know about it," said Johnson. "I told him he'd better get into the show or it's all over. I don't know why I said that. All of a sudden he said, 'I'm bringing us back,' and he did. Single-handedly."

Jordan scored one basket, then another, then another. He'd wave teammates away so he could go one-on-one, then he'd set up teammates for open shots when he was double-teamed. Quickly, Jordan's team caught up and finally edged in front 40-36 when it was over.

"I pushed him to his level, the highest that he can go," Johnson said. "I didn't like it at the time, but at the same time, I did enjoy it.

It was really something. Your mind says you want to stop him, but the other side of it says you have no chance. He just starts jumping over you. Every time I looked up, he had his shoes on my No. 15."

Said Jordan, "I'm not sure people will ever see the true greatness of this team because we may never be pressed to that level. But a little of it came out today and it was really a beautiful thing."

Jordan was accurate in predicting the Dream Team would go unchallenged, but that only adds to the team's mystique. "These 12 superstars had come together to form a super team," said Daly. "They were truly what their nickname promised—a Dream Team."

00:06

The Olympic Game That Ended Three Times

When the clock ticks down to zero and the buzzer sounds with one team in the lead, the game is over, right? Not if the officials say it isn't.

That's what happened in the gold medal game of the 1972 Olympics in Munich, Germany, when the final seconds were replayed not once but twice. As a result, what appeared to be a 50-49 victory for the United State turned into a 51-50 triumph for the Soviet Union, which handed the U.S. its first loss ever in Olympic competition.

From the time basketball was introduced as an Olympic medal sport on a dirt court in Berlin in 1936, the United States had dominated the competition. In the seven Olympiads from 1936 through 1968, the United States came home with the gold every time and did not lose a single game along the way. The 1956 team, led by Bill Russell and K.C. Jones, won its games by an average margin of 54 points, and the 1960 team, led by Oscar Robertson, Jerry West, Jerry Lucas and Walt Bellamy—four future Hall of Famers—is considered the greatest amateur basketball team ever assembled.

Note the word "amateur." Until 1992, international rules prohibited NBA players from representing the United States in the Olympics and other global competitions, although players from other countries who were paid to play ball were allowed to compete. The result of this double standard was that the United States sent teams composed of collegians or players from the industrial leagues that thrived in the 1940s and 1950s to compete against generally older and more experienced players from other countries.

"In 1972, our team averaged just 20.6 years of age, and when we played a team like the Soviet Union, it was boys against men," said Hall of Fame coach Chuck Daly, who guided the United States' Dream Team to the gold medal in 1992. "For many of us, that was truly the first realization that Americans were not the only people playing basketball. In the other Olympics, we had taken it for granted that we would win. But 1972 showed us that we were not invincible."

Even if it did take two replays of the finish to do it.

The Soviet Union led for most of the game, but with three seconds left, Doug Collins drove to the basket and was knocked to the floor by Zurab Sakandelidze. Though dazed, Collins got up and sank both free throws to give the United States a 50-49 lead. The Soviets inbounded the ball, but suddenly, play was stopped with one second left when some fans ran onto the court. When play resumed, the Soviets threw the ball off the backboard, the Americans recovered as the buzzer sounded and headed off the court to celebrate their victory.

Some five minutes later, an official of the International Basketball Federation went to the locker room and told the team to get back onto the floor. The Soviet coach apparently had requested a timeout after Collins' last free throw, and so three seconds were put back on the clock. The Soviets inbounded the ball once again, a shot was missed and the buzzer sounded, and again the Americans began to celebrate.

But once again it was premature. The timer had mistakenly set the game clock to 00:50 instead of 00:03 before play resumed, and officials ordered the ending replayed once again.

This time, Ivan Edeshko threw a court-length pass toward Aleksander Belov near the opposite free-throw line. Belov and Kevin Joyce of the United States collided while going for the ball, but no foul was called. Belov caught the pass, turned and shot, the ball going through at the buzzer. This time it was the Soviets who were celebrating, and this time the 51-50 victory stood.

The Americans protested the way the end of the game was conducted, but to no avail. They voted not to accept their silver medals, believing to this day they deserved the gold.

Collins, who later starred for the Philadelphia 76ers, coached the Chicago Bulls and Detroit Pistons and did commentary on NBC and TNT, was a member of the team that represented the United States in 1972. He remembers that game as if it were played yesterday.

"It was a very bittersweet experience for me, to be a member of the first U.S. men's basketball team to lose in the Olympics, but I still don't believe that we lost. It was something that was out of our hands," he said.

"We were down by one with about 10 seconds to go, but I was able to steal a pass and was heading for a layup when I was fouled with three seconds left. I slid under the basket and hit my head on the basket support. I was unconscious for a few seconds, and when I went to the foul line, I still felt groggy. But I think that helped me, because I didn't feel the pressure. I made two shots, and we were ahead by one.

"That's when all the confusion began. The Russians got two (extra) chances to win it, and they finally put one in and won 51-50. After being so happy about the two free throws I had made, I was the most dejected person in the world.

"I think the one thing I regret more than anything else is not having that feeling you get standing on the platform, getting the gold medal around your neck and listening to the national anthem. I feel we were robbed of that."

00:05

• •

The Greatest Game of All Time?

It's folly to try to pick one "greatest basketball game of all time" from among the millions that have taken place since Dr. Naismith had the first peach baskets nailed up in Springfield in 1891. But if pressed, more than a few basketball historians will point to the Boston Celtics' 128-126 triple-overtime victory over the Phoenix Suns in the 1976 NBA Playoffs as a game that had everything—buzzer-beating shots, high stakes, surprise heroes, innovative strategy, controversial calls and general pandemonium in the arena.

The Celtics, who won the Atlantic Division title with a 54-28 record, were a veteran team built around 6-foot-9 center Dave Cowens, 27, and guards Jo Jo White, 29, and Charlie Scott, 27. The other core players were getting on in years—Don Nelson was 36, John Havlicek 35 (and hobbled in the playoffs by an injured foot), Paul Silas 32. It also was not a deep team, with Nelson the only proven veteran on the bench.

The Suns were an eight-year-old expansion franchise that reached the NBA Finals for the first time by knocking off the defending champion Golden State Warriors in a seven-game Western Conference Final, taking Game 7 on the road 94-86. Phoenix, which had finished 17 games behind the Warriors in the Pacific Division at 42-40, featured the NBA's Rookie of the Year at center, the versatile, 6-foot-9 Alvan Adams, and a high-scoring, creative guard, Paul Westphal, who had been traded by Boston for Scott before the start of the season.

Boston was favored in the finals based on experience, as the Celtics had won the title two years earlier with much the same cast. But Phoenix had been the underdog against Golden State as well, and in Westphal, it had a budding star who had been kept on the Boston bench for three seasons and was eager to show up his former team.

The Celtics won the first two games at home rather handily, but Phoenix stepped up its intensity on its home floor and posted two close victories to even the series heading back to Boston Garden for Game 5.

It didn't start off very impressively. The Celtics raced to a 32-12 lead and appeared headed for their third home-court rout. But Phoenix closed the gap to 15 points at halftime and then limited the Celtics to 34 points in the second half, the game going into overtime, tied at 95-95, after Curtis Perry of Phoenix and Havlicek of Boston each missed two late free throws.

Each team scored six points in overtime, which ended amidst controversy when Boston had the ball and Silas signaled for a timeout in the closing seconds. The Celtics already had used up their allotment of timeouts and would have been charged with a technical foul had the timeout been granted, but referee Richie Powers ignored the request and let the final seconds tick off the clock with the score tied. The Phoenix bench was furious, since Silas was right near Powers and the referee couldn't have missed seeing the timeout request, but the game went into a second overtime.

"The second overtime was incredible," said Havlicek. "There were all kinds of great plays on both sides."

Boston moved in front and was holding a three-point lead with 19 seconds on the clock when Dick Van Arsdale scored for the Suns. Westphal then came up with a steal, and though Curtis Perry missed a medium-range jumper, he put in his own rebound to push Phoenix in front 110-109 with four seconds left.

Havlicek met Nelson's inbounds pass near mid-court on the left side and drove toward the lane. "I knew they weren't going to risk fouling me," he said. "I split two defenders and they sort of backed off. I knew I wanted to bank it, because in moving forward like that, it's a better idea. When I put it on the glass, I can be a little off and still make the basket. This one was banked really well; there wasn't any doubt about it. There was this tremendous roar, and I looked at the clock and I think there may have been one second showing, but then there were none. I assumed the game was over."

Havlicek's running bank shot from about 12 feet out gave Boston a 111-110 lead and sent hundreds of fans pouring over the courtside press tables and onto the parquet floor in a wild celebration. Amidst the tumult, referees Powers and Don Murphy could be seen blowing their whistles, waving their arms and racing over to the scorer's table, indicating that the game was not over. Although the clock had run down to zero, there was one second remaining when the ball went through the net, so they had one second put back on the clock. The court had to be cleared, and several of the Celtics, including Havlicek, had to be brought back out from the locker room, where they had gone, seeking refuge. All this took several minutes and gave the Suns—who were out of timeouts—a chance to recover from Havlicek's basket and think about a final play. It also gave Westphal time to come up with an idea.

Perhaps inspired by what had occurred at the end of the first overtime, Westphal suggested to Suns coach John MacLeod that Phoenix call a timeout and purposely draw a technical foul. While Boston would get a free-throw attempt that might stretch the lead to two points, when play resumed, the Suns would get to inbound the ball from mid-court instead of from under their own basket and thus have a better chance at what would at worst be a game-tying basket.

MacLeod bought it and White made the free throw, making Boston's lead 112-110. But Perry's pass went to forward Gar Heard, who caught it just to the right of the key and in one motion turned and arched a rainbow jumper that sailed through, the buzzer sounding while the shot was in midair. The game was tied and the Celtics were stunned, their fans deflated. In a matter of seconds, Boston Garden had gone from pandemonium to near-silence.

Cowens and Scott had fouled out by the beginning of the third overtime, and Silas fouled out during the period, but Celtics coach Tom Heinsohn found salvation from an unexpected source —little-used 6-foot-6 swingman Glenn McDonald.

"It seems that in a game like that, you always get a hero nobody counted on," observed Havlicek. "This time it was Glenn McDonald, who hadn't even played in five of the first 13 playoff games, who came in and gave us a big lift. He was fresher than most of the people on the floor and he took advantage of it by running downcourt to get to the open spots on the floor."

McDonald put the Celtics ahead to stay with a basket with 1:39 remaining in the third overtime. He also hit a fallaway jumper from the corner and a pair of free throws for a total of six points in the five-minute period.

Two free throws by backup center Jim Ard stretched Boston's lead to six points with 31 seconds left, but Westphal came back with a pair of quick baskets and suddenly it was down to two in the closing seconds. The game ended with Ard clutching the inbounds pass and the Suns trying to foul anyone they could reach, but the buzzer sounded and Boston had a 128-126 victory.

The Celtics went to Phoenix and closed out the series with an 87-80 victory in Game 6 for their 13th NBA championship, but Game 5 is the one everyone remembers from that series.

"People immediately began calling it the most exciting or best-played game they had ever seen," said Havlicek, "and I'd have to say it was the most exciting I've ever been in. There were so many highs and lows, so many times when we went from winning to losing and back to what we thought was winning again."

"I honestly thought that the game was over three different times before it really ended," said White, who sat down on the floor in exhaustion after playing 60 minutes and scoring 33 points. "Once was when we 'won it' by one point (in the second overtime) and two times when I stood under the basket and watched shots (by Perry and Heard) fall right through."

Hall of Famer Rick Barry, one of the game's broadcasters, called it "the most exciting basketball game I've ever seen. They just had one great play after another. It was such an emotional and physical game for everybody involved."

00:04

. . . .

Carlisle's Second Effort Wins NIT for California

If at first you don't succeed, get yourself a second chance and make the most of it. Geno Carlisle did and it resulted in the 1999 NIT championship for California.

With his Golden Bears trailing Clemson 60-58 and time running down, Carlisle, a 6-foot-3 senior guard, drove into the lane, only to have his shot rejected by Andrius Jurkunas. But as the ball bounded loose, Carlisle scrambled and managed to retrieve it, then drove back into the lane, put up an acrobatic shot and was fouled by Tom Wideman. As the referee's whistle blew, the ball nestled through the net with 4.7 seconds left, tying the game.

Clemson called its last timeout, but the effort to ice Carlisle was futile. He stepped to the line and calmly sank the free throw, giving California a 61-60 lead.

The Tigers had one last chance, and guard Terrell McIntyre quickly pushed the ball upcourt, but his driving attempt bounced off the rim at the buzzer. California had the win and its first postseason title since taking the NCAA crown four decades earlier, coincidentally also by a one-point margin, 71-70, over a West Virginia team that featured Jerry West.

For Carlisle, who led California with 15.9 points and 3.9 assists per game in the 1998-99 season, it was a memorable finish to an otherwise forgettable night. Prior to his game-winning three-point play, he had shot just 3-for-17 from the field. And that had come on the heels of a subpar performance in the tournament semifinals.

"I thought these last two games were my worst two games of the season," he said afterwards. "I was having a horrible game up to that point. And then it was just that moment."

And despite Carlisle's earlier misfirings, Cal coach Ben Braun was perfectly happy to have his team's fate in Carlisle's hands.

"We always want to have the ball in Geno's hands at the end of the game," said Braun. "If nothing else, he was going to try and get to the foul line. He got a little greedy, and got the basket as well."

Carlisle finished with a team-high 16 points, including 8-for-9 from the free-throw line. "I asked God to take the fear and nervousness I had in me away," he said of his trip to the line for the game-winner. "That free-throw, it was for history, it was for everything we worked for."

The victory was especially sweet for Carlisle and backcourt mate Thomas Kilgore, both of whom transferred to Cal prior to the 1997-98 season—Carlisle from Northwestern and Kilgore from Central Michigan. The Bears were on NCAA probation their first year, so their senior year provided their one and only taste of postseason play.

"These players deserve it," said Braun. "It's hard to practice when you don't have any prize to chase. But all these players practiced extremely hard last season. What happened last season made us a better basketball team."

The Bears missed a chance at an NCAA tournament berth when they were beaten by Pac-10 rival Oregon in their season finale, dropping their record to 17-11. In the NIT they rallied from 12 points behind to beat Fresno State, came from 17 points down to defeat DePaul and then topped Colorado State to earn a trip to New York for the semifinals, where they exacted revenge on Oregon with an 85-69 victory.

In the final, Clemson led by as many as eight points in the first half and by 59-56 with 1:18 left. A layup by Michael Gill brought Cal within one, but Jurkunas hit the second of two free throws to make it 60-58 with 29 seconds left. That's when Braun turned to Carlisle, and Carlisle's second effort paid off.

"We wanted him to take the ball to the basket and, hopefully, either hit the basket or draw the foul," said Braun. Carlisle got off his shot with about 10 seconds on the clock, but the 6-foot-10 Jurkunas slapped it away. The ball rolled loose near the free-throw line, where Carlisle got a hand in between Clemson's McIntyre and Harold Jamison and came up with it for his second try.

"A good or bad bounce decided the championship," said Clemson coach Larry Shyatt. "An odd bounce on a blocked shot was the difference between winning and losing."

"When I got the first shot blocked, everything then started happening in slow motion," said Carlisle. "Everything slowed down. There were two guys coming for the ball and I went to knock it back. I just knew we had to at least tie it up. I had to get in there.

"This is a perfect ending to my career."

00:03

Paxson Nails the Three-Peat

At the end of a remarkable play in which all five Chicago Bulls players on the court touched the ball, veteran guard John Paxson became the unlikely hero when he sank a three-pointer with 3.9 seconds to play, giving the Bulls a 99-98 victory over the Phoenix Suns in Game 6 of the 1993 NBA Finals and Chicago's third consecutive NBA title.

Paxson was the consummate role player whose game was overshadowed by the brilliance of Michael Jordan and the flair of Scottie Pippen, yet his spot-shooting ability made him an ideal complement to their creative genius. That skill was always there, and when he was called upon, Paxson's teammates knew what the result would be.

"Once Paxson got the ball, I knew it was over," said Jordan.

"I just caught the ball and shot it, as I have my whole life," said Paxson, whose father and brother also played in the NBA. "I've been playing basketball since I was eight years old, and I've shot like that in my driveway hundreds of thousands of times. It was just reaction."

Phoenix Suns coach Paul Westphal, a prolific scorer in his playing days, was bitterly disappointed at the play that ended the

Suns' championship dream. But still he could step back and appreciate the moment, knowing what it had to feel like for Paxson.

"I just had to smile to myself," he said after the game. "It's a shot every kid dreams about. John Paxson got to live that dream out."

The dream came at a perfect time for the Bulls in their quest for a third consecutive crown. Chicago had taken three of the first four games of the finals, but had failed to close out Phoenix at home, losing Game 5 108-98. That sent the series back to Phoenix with the Bulls holding a 3-2 lead, but the Suns enjoying home-court advantage.

The Bulls dominated most of the game and led 87-79 going into the fourth quarter, but suddenly went cold, failing to score in 6:09 as the Suns rallied. Phoenix pulled in front 98-94 with 2:23 left, and with the prospect of a Game 7 at America West Arena looming large, Chicago's bid to three-peat seemed very much in jeopardy. It looked like the series was going to go the distance and that momentum had shifted to the Suns.

But after neither team scored for more than a minute, Jordan grabbed a rebound and went the length of the court to score and cut the lead in half with 38 seconds left. When Phoenix tried to milk the clock, the only shot it could get off against Chicago's smothering defense was an air ball by Dan Majerle. The 24-second violation turned the ball back over to Chicago with 14.1 seconds left.

As the Bulls came back onto the floor following a timeout, everyone in America West Arena expected Jordan to be the one to take the final shot. But Chicago coach Phil Jackson was keeping his options open—he had three guards on the floor, Paxson and B.J. Armstrong joining Jordan, plus forwards Pippen and Horace Grant. All were good shooters and all could handle the ball, leaving little opportunity for the Suns defenders to double-team or trap.

What unfolded was the kind of play coaches dream about, a play where all five players handled the ball, had the defense scrambling and finally produced a wide-open shot for one of the most precise shooters in the league. It's the kind of thing coaches fantasize about when they are alone with their chalkboards, scribbling their Xs and Os, never dreaming it could possibly be executed as well as it was in this pressure-filled situation.

Jordan inbounded the ball to Armstrong, took a return pass and brought the ball upcourt. Just when everyone expected him to accelerate to the basket, and the Phoenix defenders started to cheat over toward him to close off that option, Jordan passed off to Pippen. He quickly found Grant along the baseline, but Grant had been having a poor shooting game and wasn't eager to force a shot in traffic, even if he was only six feet from the hoop. By now the Phoenix defenders were scrambling all over the floor, and Grant found Paxson spotting up along the three-point arc on the left side.

It was catch and shoot, just what Paxson does best.

"I got a clean look at it," he said. "There was no one around me and it felt good when it left. I just caught the ball and shot it—as I have my whole life."

Paxson's three-pointer sailed through the net with 3.9 seconds remaining and gave the Bulls a 99-98 lead. Phoenix had one last chance, but when Kevin Johnson tried to drive the lane, the ball was slapped away by Grant and time ran out. Chicago had its three-peat, thanks to a shot Paxson had been shooting all his life.

"It was like a dream come true," he said. "You're a kid out in your driveway, shooting shots to win championships. When you get down to it, it's still just a shot in a basketball game. But I think a lot of people could relate to that experience."

00:02

· ·

Magic Borrows Kareem's Shot

Magic Johnson was known for his ballhandling rather than his shooting, but if you play the game of basketball long enough, especially with teammates like Kareem Abdul-Jabbar, you pick up a trick or two over time.

For years Johnson watched Abdul-Jabbar position himself in the low post, wait as players cut past him, then wheel to the basket for his favorite shot, the sky-hook, so labeled by former Milwaukee Bucks broadcaster Eddie Doucette because it seemed to rain down out of the sky toward the basket. Most of the time Abdul-Jabbar would move across the middle and into the lane before releasing the shot, but sometimes he would go in the other direction, toward the baseline and away from traffic. Either way, Abdul-Jabbar's trademark weapon helped him lead his teams to three collegiate championships at UCLA and six professional titles, one with the Milwaukee Bucks and five with the Los Angeles Lakers.

When Johnson, then a fresh-faced 20-year-old coming off an NCAA title in his sophomore year at Michigan State, joined the Lakers in the fall of 1979, Abdul-Jabbar was already 32 years old and a 10-year NBA veteran. But the youngster with the smile that could light up a building seemed to inject new life into the venerable center, and together they would form one of basketball's most successful partnerships.

On the court, Johnson's passing wizardry ensured that Abdul-Jabbar would get the ball where he wanted it and when he wanted it. Johnson's playmaking abilities literally added years to Abdul-Jabbar's career and made the second half of his tenure in the NBA far more productive than it would otherwise have been. Off the court, Johnson's proficiency with the media deflected the spotlight from the introspective center who was never comfortable in its glare, a not insignificant benefit to his presence.

Together, Abdul-Jabbar and Johnson became the heart of the NBA's Team of the Decade for the 1980s, the "Showtime" Los Angeles Lakers, a team whose glamorous style and flashy play captured the imagination of Tinseltown.

If the Lakers seemed to symbolize the glitter of the West Coast, the Boston Celtics of the 1980s were their alter ego, capturing the grit of the old-line cities of the East Coast. With Larry Bird as their Magic man, the tradition-steeped Celtics underwent a revival of their own in the 1980s, going from 29 wins the previous season to 61 wins in Bird's rookie season of 1979-80 and then winning the NBA championship in 1981.

The Lakers and Celtics of the 1980s formed one of sports' greatest rivalries. They only met twice during the regular season, but each game was a nationally televised event that attracted media from around the country and that the players approached as if a championship were at stake.

In fact, they did meet three times when the NBA championship was at stake, the Celtics winning in seven games in 1984, the Lakers winning in six games in 1985. The 1987 NBA Finals was the rubber match, the third and final time these two great teams would contest a title.

The Lakers easily won the first two games at home, but Boston came back to take Game 3 at Boston Garden. That set up Game

4 as a pivotal one, because a Boston victory would even the series, while a Laker win would put the Celtics squarely behind the eight ball, down 3-1 with two of the potential remaining three games in Los Angeles.

Spurred by the ever-noisy crowd in the old arena on Causeway Street, the Celtics built a 16-point halftime lead. But the Lakers whittled away at it until they were within eight points with three minutes left, then closed the gap to 103-102 with 30 seconds to play. Magic and Kareem ran a pick-and-roll to perfection, Abdul-Jabbar scoring to put Los Angeles in front, but Larry Bird answered with a three-point bomb to put Boston back on top 106-104 with 12 seconds left. On the next possession, the ball went inside to Abdul-Jabbar, who was fouled. He made the first free throw and missed the second, failing in his attempt to tie the game, but the rebound squirted out of bounds off Boston, giving the Lakers one more chance.

Following a timeout called by Lakers coach Pat Riley to plot a final play, Johnson took the inbounds pass near the left sideline. He thought about launching a jumper, but Kevin McHale, 6-11 with gangly arms, stood in his way. So he dribbled to his right toward the key, with McHale in pursuit and Bird and Robert Parish moving over to help out. Before they could converge on him at the foul line, however, Johnson launched a 1950s-style running hook shot that nestled through the net, giving the Lakers the lead with two seconds left to play. After a Boston timeout, Bird somehow managed to shake loose for a jumper, but it was off target as the horn sounded, and the Lakers had a 107-106 victory. The Celtics stayed alive for one more game, but the Lakers wrapped up the championship by winning Game 6 in Los Angeles 106-93.

Moments after Game 4 was over, amidst the tumult and the shouting in the Lakers' locker room, Johnson was asked to describe his game-winning shot. "That was my junior, junior sky-hook," he said, referring to Abdul-Jabbar's favorite weapon.

Down the sweaty corridor, in the Boston locker room, Bird just shook his head. "You expect to lose to the Lakers on a sky-hook," he said. "You don't expect it to be from Magic."

00:01

. . . .

Laettner's Miracle Shot Beats Kentucky

Time was running out on Duke's bid for a repeat national championship and a fifth straight trip to the Final Four. Kentucky, having watched a 15-foot jumper by Duke point guard Bobby Hurley that would have decided the 1992 East Regional final in regulation rim out, was leading 103-102 in overtime after Sean Woods drove past Hurley and banked home a 12-footer.

Duke called a timeout with 2.1 seconds left. Tears were in the eyes of Duke coach Mike Krzyzewski's daughter, Debbie; his wife, Mickie, sat next to her in the stands at the Spectrum in Philadelphia, her head bowed. They could sense the end of Duke's championship reign. But Coach K's confidence never wavered, and the Duke players picked up on it.

"No matter what situation we were in, he was confident," said Duke forward Grant Hill. "We all came to the huddle still burned by the shot that put Kentucky up, and Coach K had a plan already mapped out on the board. He said, 'Okay, here's how we win the game: Grant, you throw to Christian here and he'll take the shot to win.' And that's exactly how it happened."

It was a play that just about every team has in its playbook, and one that just about never works—because not every team has players like Hill and Christian Laettner to execute it.

As Hill prepared to take the ball out of bounds under his own basket, Laettner set up at the foul line at the opposite end of the Spectrum in Philadelphia, his back to the basket. Once Hill was handed the ball, the lanky, 6-foot-11 Laettner—three inches taller than any Kentucky player on the floor—spread out his arms to give his teammate as large a target as possible.

Hill winged a baseball pass some 75 feet, his aim dead on. Kentucky's John Pelphrey made a move to try to intercept the pass, then backed off, fearing a foul call that would send Laettner to the line, where he already was a perfect 10-for-10. Then again, maybe he should have taken his chances, for Laettner hadn't missed any of his nine field goal tries, either.

Laettner caught the pass with his back to the hoop, faked to his right, then took one dribble as he spun to his left. Pelphrey was off balance and Deron Feldhaus of Kentucky was anchored to the floor, too slow to react, as Laettner rose up and shot a 16-foot, right-handed jumper that seemed to hang in the air for several seconds before going through the net.

"Totally incredible—I didn't even see it go in," said Laettner, who was engulfed by a swarm of Duke players and fans.

Over on the Duke sideline, Coach Krzyzewski had a different angle but the same view, or non-view. "As soon as he let it go, I knew it was going in," he said, "but I didn't see it because everyone jumped in front of me."

"I wanted them to make a lucky jump shot, a prayer," said Kentucky coach Rick Pitino—only this time Duke's prayer was answered.

Laettner's miraculous shot brought back memories of his game-winning jumper against Connecticut at the Meadowlands two years earlier that sent Duke to the Final Four.

"This seemed to take a lot longer than that shot," said Laettner, the first collegian ever to start in four Final Fours and the holder of the NCAA Tournament career scoring record of 407 points. "I had a lot more time to think. It was totally incredible. This is more fun than the Connecticut game because it's the second time. I can't believe it would be a better feeling, but it was."

Laettner's ability to repeatedly come through in the clutch was no surprise to his coach.

"Christian has this hunger for competition that I've never seen in anybody else," said Krzyzewski. "He's never afraid to make the play, be it a shot, rebound, pass, block, whatever. He wants to be there when the game is decided.

"You've heard of guys who burn to win? This guy's got a forest fire inside him."

Laettner's turnaround jumper against Kentucky ended one of the most remarkable games in college basketball history between two of the nation's most successful programs and high-profile coaches. Duke led 50-45 after a fast-paced first half and seemed to be cruising with a 12-point advantage shortly before Laettner, the winner of the Wooden, Kodak and Naismith awards as college basketball's Player of the Year, was fouled by Aminu Timberlake of Kentucky. Timberlake fell to the floor, and as Laettner crossed over him, he stepped on the Kentucky player's stomach, drawing a technical foul.

Kentucky, using a pressure defense and the scoring of Jamaal Mashburn and Dale Brown, came roaring back, scoring nine straight points in one stretch to tie the score at 81-81 with 5:27 to play. "We got in our press, turned them over and Mash hit a couple of threes," said the Wildcats' Jimmy Farmer.

It was close the rest of the way, with Duke taking a 93-91 lead with 1:02 on the clock on a jumper by Thomas Hill and Kentucky tying the score when Feldhaus converted a Pelphrey miss with 38.6 seconds left. Hurley missed a driving jumper with two seconds left and the teams went into overtime, where they slugged it out like two heavyweights in the 15th round of a title fight.

Pelphrey hit a three-pointer at 3:58 and Hurley answered with a trey at 2:40. Pelphrey sank two free throws at 2:17, Laettner matched them at 1:53, then put Duke up 100-98 with a running eight-footer with 31.5 seconds left. Mashburn, Kentucky's All-American, responded by converting a three-point play on a driving layup, giving the Wildcats a one-point lead with 19.6 seconds left. But Mashburn fouled out on the next play, and Laettner went to the line and converted two more free throws for a 102-101 lead with 14.1 showing on the clock. Kentucky called a timeout with 7.2 seconds left to set up Woods' basket, which paved the way for the dramatic finish.

"It was a rare game, truly one of the best I've ever seen," said Georgia Tech coach Bobby Cremins. "Laettner's incredible, absolutely incredible. He never ceases to amaze you."

"I don't know if I can find the right words to do the game justice," offered Wake Forest coach Dave Odom. "On the play at the end, it was a great pass and a great catch. But once those two are completed, you've got to have—*will* is not a strong enough word—one of the strongest constitutions in all of sport to take and make that shot."

"I can't believe it. Did that just happen?" Krzyzewski said in the interview room moments afterwards. "There aren't enough adjectives to describe it. You can't write enough to tell about all the great plays that were made in that game."

Laettner, who hit every shot he attempted, led all scorers with 31 points as Duke shot a sizzling .654 (34-for-52) from the field, including .500 (8-for-16) from three-point range, and .824 (28-

for-34) from the foul line. Hurley added 22 points and 10 assists, Thomas Hill had 19 points, and Grant Hill contributed 11 points, 10 rebounds and 7 assists. Mashburn had 28 points and 10 rebounds and Woods had 21 points and 9 assists for Kentucky, which shot .569 percent from the field, including 12-for-22 from three-point range, to keep the pressure on all the way.

"Against some teams you can make a mistake and not have it hurt you, but not against Kentucky," said Laettner. "They punish you every single time."

In the end, however, it was Laettner who punished the Wildcats.

"I told the kids in the locker room, I think we've just been a part of history," said Krzyzewski. "It's got to be somewhere in (David) Letterman's Top 10. You can't simulate these moments."

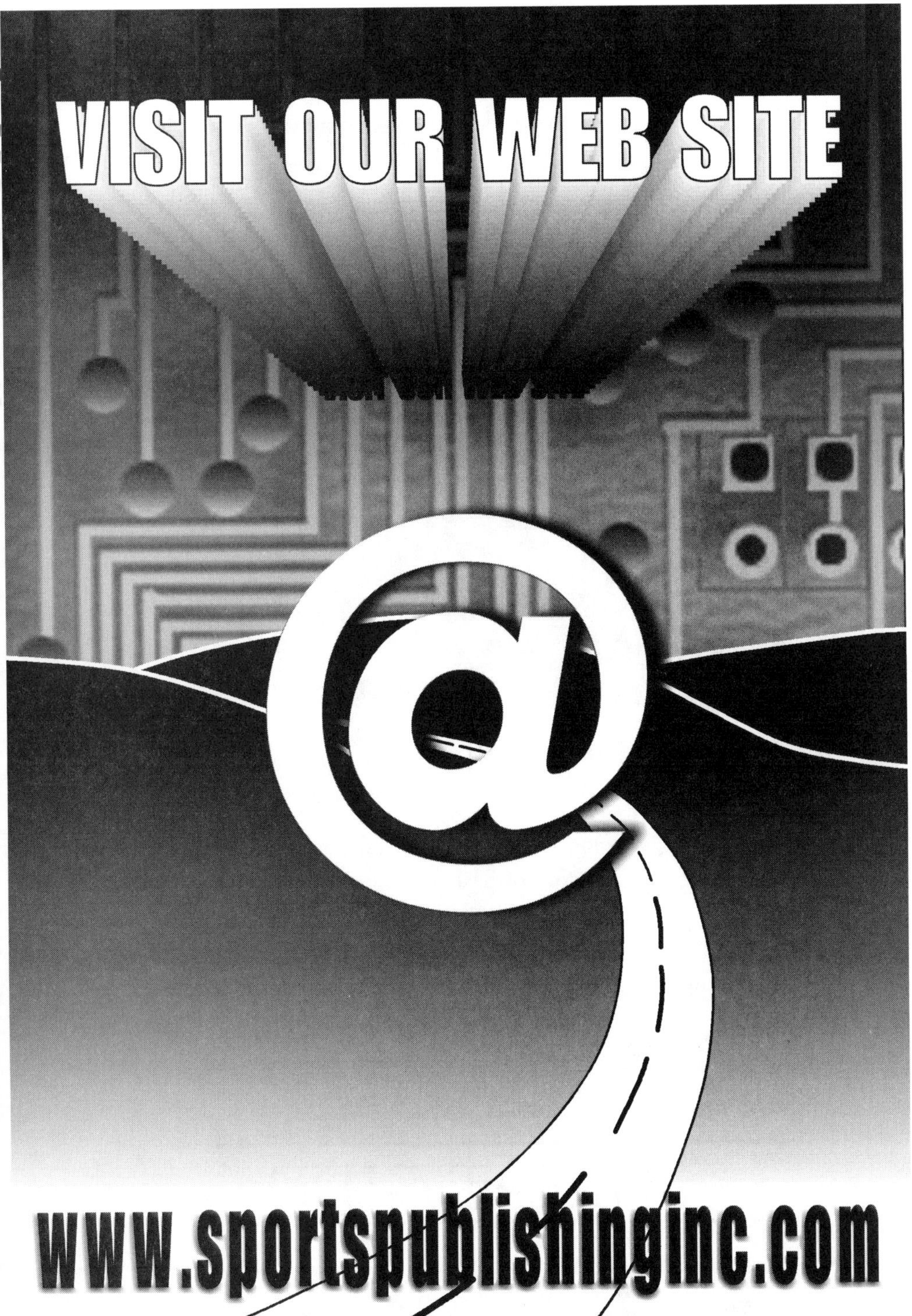
VISIT OUR WEB SITE
www.sportspublishinginc.com

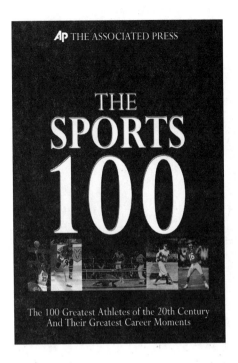

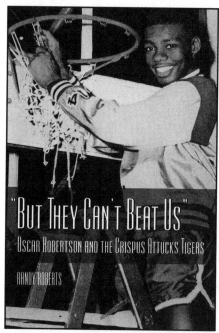